# Divine Purpose

## The 13 Principles of Ascension

## Lysa Black

Also by the Author:

*Heart Healing:*

*The 13 Principles of Emotional Self Healing*

Divine Purpose: The 13 Principles of Ascension

By Lysa Black

Published by
Transcendent Publishing
P.O. Box 66202
St. Pete Beach, FL 33736
www.transcendentpublishing.com

Transcendent
——Publishing——

ISBN-10: 0-9993125-0-2
ISBN-13: 978-0-9993125-0-6
Printed in the United States of America.

# Dedication

To the beautiful souls who have known

the depths of descent,

may you rise in all your glory.

# Acknowledgements

To my beloved clients – each of you inspires me beyond measure. This book wouldn't have been possible without each and every one of you. Thank you for granting me permission to witness your lives and enter your hearts. Your courage and purity moves me deeply! I'm humbled and in awe of you all.

To my husband, Abinadi Black, who stood by me and was the gentle reassuring love I needed daily – thank you. You always believe in me and remind me to trust myself. Witnessing your commitment to honour your truth has been a spectacular journey to behold, you are the harbinger of so much joy and love in my life! Thank you for being my miracle!

To my divine children, Orion and Bow; you both radiate your truth so powerfully that it's unmistakable. I'm continually in awe of the magnificence of you both. Thank you for helping me to remember my own purity and potency.

To Bronwyn Bay - without you as my editor I would have been lost and frustrated. Being able to pour out these stories, ideas and feelings and then trust you to arrange them and lift them to a beautiful reading order has been a massive blessing for me. Knowing someone was working by my side to see this book come to life has given it the investment of love and care that it's required. If this is my baby, you've definitely been a midwife – thank you, beautiful!

To Katie Shumack - I'm very grateful to receive your enthusiastic support in final proofing. Your attention to details and recommendations were excellent. Thank you for expressing your joy in reading this book, it helped me in the final hours.

To Carin Newbould - I felt like you were right beside me in the final hours of proofing. Being able to receive your support meant the world to me – Thank you for being so dependable and passionate!

To Karina Ladet - you are a real earth angel! I'm deeply grateful that you came into my life and always knew exactly what to say; you showed me that I truly am worth being with and whispered timely heavenly assurance in my own moments of doubt. Without your display of love, my heart would not have had the stamina to continue.

To Ruby Toad, you are a wise earth magic wielding wonder! Thank you for the sacred guidance I required to permit myself to rise into my divine purpose; thank you for showing up and holding me to the divinity within.

To Lara Waldman, your commitment to expansion gave me the impetus to feel safe in my desires. Thank you for your embodiment of divinity; you're a breath-taking wonder to behold.

To my Kiwi Biz Mastermind Babes: Natalie Cutler-Welsh, Natalie Tolhopf and Kim Baird - thank you for supporting me to own my genius, and feel safe progressing in my purpose and business. Each of you is showing up so spectacularly, it makes 'changing the world' feel like just another daily to-do item!

To Soulful Skyler Mechelle, you popped into my life at exactly the right time to lift, lighten and support my soul work. I'm incredibly blessed to know the magnitude of your soul and knowing you comprehend me brings a wash of deep appreciation from my tender heart.

To my heavenly parents, you both loved me first. You trusted me to endure my own descent for the sake of preparing the way for my ascent. Your tender devotion, unmistakable guidance and infinite love carries me through.

# Contents

# Foreword

More often than we realise, spirit leads us to a person, a moment, an opportunity that opens our hearts and invites us to rise. Lysa Black is one of these people, and your choice to pick up her book, *Divine Purpose*, is one of these opportunities.

Lysa has a powerful ability to see into the hearts of people; to intuitively call out their gifts and invite them to know themselves in deep and magnificent ways. This is her divine purpose. One that she rose into as she ascended out of the depths of her own darkness and found her home on the mountains; calling women to step into their unique and beautiful freedom alongside her. She is a leader who walks, feels and chooses ascension in every inch of her being. Her divine purpose to raise women into their birthright, is rooted in her own choice to answer spirit's leadings. She rose, so she can now raise.

*Divine Purpose* is not just a book, and Lysa Black is not just a woman. The truths in this book, offered through Lysa's powerful voice, will invite you on a journey that will change your life forever. Freedom has no expiration date, and the choice to ascend is eternal. It is a lifelong choice that begins with a single "yes" and crescendos out into a ripple effect that awakens all of who you are and all of who you are called to be. Here is the first step of many. Here is the first taste of what it means for you to own your birthright. Here is your story and truth, reclaimed not erased. Here is where you rise.

Welcome home, sister, welcome home.

*Skyler Mechelle*

# The Ascension of Ishtar

*This is the sacred story of Ishtar, the Goddess of fertility. The story of how she fell into grief and unknowingly gave away her power. She allowed herself to lose her light before reclaiming it and ascending from the depths to rise in divine purpose.*

After losing her beloved husband Tammuz, the still young Ishtar was heartbroken and stricken with grief. Her advances toward the great King Gilgamesh were rejected and Ishtar was left feeling deeply depressed and hopeless. She decided to seek out her dearly departed husband Tammuz in the dark underworld of the dead, a kingdom ruled by her sister Irkalla.

Ishtar began her descent into the underworld through the passage of a cave. Within that cave stood seven walls with seven gates. Ishtar cried out "Let me in". The guardian of the gate, Nadu, peered over at her.

"Open this gate, or I will break it down and release all the dead to the land above and they will consume all of the living." Ishtar demanded.

Nadu replied "Please don't break down the gate, let me take your request to her Majesty Irkalla, Queen of the Underworld. Wait until I return".

When Irkalla received word of her sister's request she was enraged. "How dare she come down into my kingdom? I'll teach her a lesson!"

Irkalla commanded that Nadu grant Ishtar passage into the underworld.

Nadu returned and unbolted the locks and opened the first gate saying "You may enter the realm of Irkalla, fine lady. Welcome to the place from which no one returns" and as he spoke he took Ishtar's head piece.

"Why are you taking my head piece?" Ishtar asked.

"Tis the wish of Lady Irkalla. You may only enter if you submit to her rule" Nadu explained, so Ishtar bent her head and passed through the first gate. Shortly she came to the second gate and once again Nadu unlocked the bolts and opened the second gate. He removed the star necklace adorning her throat and when Ishtar asked "What are you doing?" Nadu replied, "Tis the wish of Lady Irkalla, you may only enter if you submit to her rule."

Nadu went on to unlock the third gate and removed the gold bracelets from Ishtar's wrists, declaring "Tis the wish of Lady Irkalla. You may only enter if you submit to her rule."

At the fourth gate, Nadu granted her access only after removing the golden belt from her waist. Ishtar passed through and once again at the fifth gate, Nadu removed her jewel encrusted girdle. At the sixth gate, Nadu removed Ishtar's shoes from her feet, and at the seventh gate, passage was granted only as Ishtar was stripped naked. Ishtar had lost all of her Goddess adornment and now stood exposed, completely naked.

She finally entered the realm of Irkalla and stood bewildered before her sister, the Queen of the Underworld. Behind Irkalla's throne the dead gathered, with no light in their eyes. The dead were dressed in black feathers and their arms had become the wings of birds. Ishtar became frightened, wishing she had not come to this dark place in search of her beloved husband Tammuz. Her quest was hopeless and now she was trapped. Desperate and afraid, she bowed before Irkalla pleading for her freedom. Irkalla decreed, "You are in my realm now. No one returns from the underworld. The gates are already bolted behind you!"

Irkalla sent forth a venomous snake to transform the Goddess

Ishtar into a black bird. With one venomous bite, Ishtar became covered in black feathers and within moments the light from her eyes extinguished, as all of her memories and hope for Tammuz went out.

High above on the earth, a great change came as Ishtar's light was lost in the underworld. Love, affection and the desire for procreation ceased in man and animal in the absence of the goddess of fertility. Birds stopped singing, bulls no longer searched for cows, stallions lost attraction to their mares, and rams cared not for ewes. Wives ceased to receive their husbands.

Shamash, the Sun God, was deeply troubled by what he saw. He knew of the disaster that would ensue if procreation ceased; it was only a matter of time. While Shamash knew his power could not rival Irkalla's strength, he turned to Ea, the Great God and shared how earth's creatures were no longer renewing themselves. Ea decided to form Udush, a creature devoid of any emotion or fear, to act as a powerful emissary to restore Ishtar and return life to earth. Ea sent Udush deep into the underworld where he effortlessly passed through the seven gates much to the surprise of Nadu. He stood in the court of Irkalla and announced "I am here for Ishtar, the Goddess of Fertility".

Irkalla stood and screamed, attempting to scare and curse Udush, but her powers were no match for the great God Ea and Udush withstood the blow unaffected. Irkalla was bound to submit and she brought forth Ishtar covered in feathers. All watched as Udush administered the waters of life, sprinkling it over her black feathers. They saw her transform back to her natural form.

Ishtar was restored; however, she was weaker than a new born babe. Although diminished, she had life once more. Udush guided her through the darkness as she ascended through each of the seven gates. Nadu saw Ishtar feebly drawing near and held out her dress and guided her through the seventh gate. At the sixth gate he replaced her shoes. At the fifth gate, her jewel encrusted girdle was returned, as was her golden belt at the fourth gate. Nadu placed Ishtar's golden bracelets rightly upon her wrists at the third gate, and her precious star necklace at the second. Back at the first gate, Ishtar bent her head down and Nadu placed her headpiece shining in full glory upon her precious head and she arose returned to her magnificence with renewed life and power.

As Ishtar came forward from the cave entrance to walk upon the earth, the stallion bolted toward the mare, the bull reared for the cow, and rams went in pursuit of ewes. Men fled homes into the loving arms of their wives; all of creation rejoiced.

*Adapted from:*

*http://fairytalesoftheworld.com/quick-reads/ishtars-journey-into-the-underworld/*

# What is Divine Purpose?

*Our divine purpose is to embody and radiate the truth of who we are. Ishtar's story is a rite of passage, outlining how we can retrieve the truth from each of our chakra centres and rise in full power.*

All of us have experienced a devastating loss, just as Ishtar did. As we tumble down into grief, we all go through a process of giving away our truth in a desperate bid to alleviate our loss.

As we give over sacred portions of our truth in an attempt to escape our pain, we descend further. By rejecting, forgetting, hiding and disowning the attributes that make us who we are, we ultimately betray ourselves.

We will all experience a descent that will ultimately extinguish our light. That's when spirit swoops in and begins leading and guiding us home to the full measure of our being. As we reclaim the truth from each of our power centres we transcend our suffering, align with our sacred purpose and reunite with our divinity.

Allowing ourselves to be purposefully led to retrieve the sacred truth we unknowingly gave away becomes the path of our ascension. Our divine purpose is to consecrate the pain of forgetting and rejecting our truth and turn it into our triumphant return to the glory of embodying our divinity.

Every one of us is a divine being incarnate. We have all forgotten the truth of who we truly are. Forgetting who we are brings about a type of living death that can become the initiation of our re-birth. Through gifts of the spirit, we are brought back to life and stumble with feeble legs to finally realise the sacredness and power of simply being exactly who we are. That's when our divine purpose is activated. That's when we begin our sacred quest to embody our truth - just as Ishtar did - and rise in our full power.

Coming out of the shadow lands of loss and grief is our common path. Being broken open, we ultimately become humble and receptive, allowing spirit within to heal, guide and lead us. The more we are able to heal, reclaim and re-integrate truth into our power centres, the more light and love we can hold. The more light and love we can hold, the more easily we can embody our truth and fulfil our divine purpose.

# The Seven Gates

First Gate – **Ishtar's Headpiece –**

The Third Eye Chakra

| *Wounded perspective* | *Healed perspective* |
|---|---|
| **I do not know what to believe** | **I see the truth** |
| **There has been a big mistake** | **I see perfection** |
| **Nothing makes sense** | **I see divine love** |

Second Gate – **Ishtar's Star Necklace –**

Throat Chakra

| *Wounded perspective* | *Healed perspective* |
|---|---|
| **No one will believe me** | **I speak my truth** |
| **I'm not allowed to share** | **I express myself** |
| **I cannot speak** | **I share clearly** |

Third Gate – **Ishtar's Golden Bracelets** –

Heart Chakra

| *Wounded perspective* | *Healed perspective* |
|---|---|
| **I don't know love** | **I love freely** |
| **Love is weakness** | **I receive love easily** |
| **There is not enough love** | **I share love generously** |

Fourth Gate – **Ishtar's Golden belt** –

Solar Plexus

| *Wounded perspective* | *Healed perspective* |
|---|---|
| **I can't create what I want** | **I own my power** |
| **I'm lost** | **I know who I am** |
| **I'm not allowed** | **I desire what's** |
| **what I want** | **intended for me** |

Fifth Gate – **Ishtar's Jewel Encrusted Girdle** –

Sacral Chakra

| *Wounded perspective* | *Healed perspective* |
|---|---|
| **I am disgusting** | **I am divinely sensual** |
| **It's wrong to be desirable** | **I embrace my sensuality** |
| **Sex is dirty and bad** | **I find bliss in sexual embrace** |

Sixth Gate – **Ishtar's Shoes** –

Root Chakra

| *Wounded perspective* | *Healed perspective* |
|---|---|
| **I don't know who I am** | **I am at home in my soul** |
| **I don't fit in** | **I belong here** |
| **I don't know where I belong** | **I am safe and at home in love** |

Seventh Gate – **Ishtar's dress** -

Crown Chakra

| *Wounded perspective* | *Healed perspective* |
|---|---|
| **I'm shut-off and alone** | **I open to receive** |
| **I'm afraid of myself** | **I am divine** |
| **No one can help me** | **I am guided at** |
| | **every turn** |

# Chapter 1:

# Descent Precedes

# Ascent

*No mud*

*No lotus.*

*Thich Nhat Hanh*

*Just as Ishtar emerges triumphant, returned and reunited with her full power and divinity, each of us is on our own sacred journey to return to our truth. This book is intended to become a sacred guide, illuminating the path for you to rise in your divine purpose. It is my hope that it will support you to find greater ease, insight and inspiration as you devote yourself to your ascension.*

From the moment this story found me, it enchanted me. The story of Ishtar is unlike any other story, as it clarifies the necessity of our descent and the possible ascent available to us all. This story points to the power and divinity of our truth and inherent purpose. I felt drawn to share it with you so that we can use this framework to support our ascension.

I have been blessed for 8 years to professionally serve women who are ascending from their own grief to reclaim their power and purpose. I have been privileged to witness their grief and come to accept what a common experience it is. In fact, I have yet to meet a soul past the age of 18 who has not experienced significant grief and loss. The women I serve would tell me how once they had given their power away and felt empty and lost within, an unseen force would enter their lives guiding, nudging and leading them forward. I noticed that those who allowed themselves to retrieve their truth and heal each specific chakra centre made swift and magical progress. They saw healing miracles confirming their own progress on their path of ascension.

I have felt inspired to seek inspiring and noble stories of women I have been blessed to work with, each of whom are well acquainted with the descent of grief. Being able to stand by them and witness how they allowed spirit to lead them to retrieve their truth has been awe-inspiring for me. I have requested permission from 11 key individuals who best represented the sacred principles of ascension that we can use to support and clarify our rise home to our divine purpose. Each of these women are heroines to me, and while their names have been changed, the details I reveal in these stories are true. Each client has been given an alias name and has personally approved their story, so that I can now relay it to you. They all expressed great joy in knowing that these private and sacred stories could reach you; all are remarkable women who have been willing to share some of the most private and intimate moments of their lives to support me in reaching you.

## What we can learn from Ishtar's story?

- Our ascent is always preceded by a descent.

- Grief is the common point initiating our descent.

- We all give our power away to some degree to gate keepers.

- We all reach a point at which we feel our light has been extinguished.

- When we feel a sense of spiritual death, spirit swoops in to reclaim us.

- Being led by spirit, we ascend and reclaim our power.

- Knowing the consequence of giving away our power, reclaiming our truth creates a sense of devotion to honouring the truth of who we are.

- The seven gates hold significance for every soul's path of ascension.

- Our divine purpose is to embody the radiant truth of who we truly are.


In my own life, I can recognise the descent and devastating loss that extinguished my light. I saw how it ushered in a period of deep reliance on spirit. It was the guidance and grace of spirit which led me to retrieve sacred portions of my truth and find myself connected once more to my divine purpose. Being led to heal my own anxiety, binge eating and pattern of break-ups taught me the value of surrendering the ideas I had about who I thought I was. I felt inspired to use the power of Ishtar's story to share a pathway that can offer clarity, comfort and guidance along our healing journey.

Just as Ishtar lost her light and went through a spiritual death, I remember a time when I felt as though I had died within. I feel a deep affinity with Ishtar's path and would like to briefly share how my life mirrors that of Ishtar. You see, I too gave away all of my power until I felt my light extinguish within. And yet I was retrieved. Spirit swooped in and grace brought me back, step by step, returning through my own gates to retrieve my truth.

I believed I had lost my Mother's love. The older I became, the less affection I received from her. The idea that she couldn't love me sent me spinning and reeling into the deepest grief I have ever known. In seeking that which I believed I had lost, I began systematically giving my truth away.

## Ishtar's Head Piece · The third eye

### *Seeing truth and divine love*

Just as Ishtar lost her crown, I lost my ability to see truth and know divine love. Once I had held the view that the world was a loving, kind and nurturing place. Over time, that view was shattered, as I believed the love I sought did not exist.

## The Star Necklace · The Throat Chakra

### *Speaking my truth*

Just as Ishtar lost her star necklace, I stopped myself from speaking the truth I knew. I began to hide my intensely bright and loving nature, in case anyone realised how desperately I needed and wanted to be loved.

## The Golden Bracelets · The Heart Chakra

### *Giving and receiving love in harmony*

Just as Ishtar lost her gold bracelets, I stopped giving and receiving love. I started to withdraw my love from those I sought to punish for their decision to retract love from me.

## The Gold Belt · Solar Plexus

### *Home of our emotions and willpower*

Just as Ishtar lost her gold belt, I stopped acknowledging what I desired. I rejected the world of emotion within me. I was swimming daily in a deep sense of misery and hopelessness that I chose to ignore. I pretended that I could not feel and allowed myself to become completely inhibited to act on any desires.

## The Jewel Encrusted Girdle · The Sacral Chakra

### Sensuality and creativity

Just as Ishtar lost her girdle, I gave up the idea that any man could ever love me. I rejected my desire to be held and feel connected intimately. I held deep shame for my body and blamed it for not being attractive enough to entitle me to experience intimacy.

## The Shoes · Root Chakra

### Belonging and safety

Just as Ishtar lost her shoes, I lived in fear of the unloving world I had trained myself to imagine. I never felt rested - only jolted and rushed by fear. I didn't fit in anywhere, especially not within myself; self-loathing ruled my inner world.

## The Dress · Crown Chakra

### Higher Connection and source of insight and truth

Just as Ishtar was stripped naked, losing her dress, I lost touch with my divine sense of connection with the heavens. I felt abandoned, alone and disconnected from life. There was no solace, no higher guidance or sense of purpose left in my being.

## My spiritual death:

At the age of 23, I phoned my Mum in an attempt to process the depth of pain that had emerged. I was desperately lost and sought to understand my first two decades of loveless life. My desire for clarity, connection and dialogue on the past was rejected, as Mum stated that she was unable to discuss what had happened. She warned that if I persisted in requesting to talk about the past, she would hang up. Yet still I pleaded… and as she hung up, I felt a final confirming blow that her love for me was truly gone. It was irretrievable and I was plunged into writhing pain and deep darkness as I seemed to fall deeply within myself. Minutes later, and I was still breathing and found myself held in grace. I was floating, as though I was suspended in some new awareness of grace; that I still lived, despite encountering the reality of my deepest fear.

In that moment, I was saved by heavenly love as it swept in to retrieve me. Slowly it led me back to embark upon a journey that would return me to my truth, my divine purpose.

I am here to support you to find out where you are on the continuum that Ishtar's story represents. If you are reading this book today, you have already experienced your light being extinguished. You are being led by spirit back up through the seven gates - the seven chakras. You are well on your way to retrieving back your power and learning how to hold your truth in honour to fully embody your divine purpose.

This book is intended as a guide to support you on your path of ascension. Writing this book has been a deeply challenging but rich experience for me, requiring every moment of writing and each stage of development to be divinely inspired and led. I have learnt and changed so much in the nine month writing process and while I am still integrating and incorporating the guidance that this book was born to reveal, it's my sincerest desire that this book can reach your precious heart.

May we both have patience with ourselves as we find our way. May we lavish ourselves with compassion and forgiveness, so that we can rise up and embody the full power and potency of our divine truth.

# Healing Guidance

1. Which part of Ishtar's story do you feel you connect with most in your life right now?

2. Which chakra have you found yourself paying conscious or unconscious attention to in your life right now?

3. What is the one area where you desire to rise higher in your life right now?

## Visualisation:

*To bring loving awareness to your soul within, allow yourself to see a pure white lotus beginning to emerge from the mud beneath. Watch it pass through the mud and water to bloom in full radiance upon the water's surface.*

| *Wounded perspective* | *Healed perspective* |
| --- | --- |
| **I can't come back from this** | **I am rising** |
| **All is lost** | **I can heal** |
| **I don't know who I am** | **I am safe in my truth** |

# Healing Affirmations

- I am the lotus

- I allow myself to be led

- I trust the heavens to guide me

- I hold myself in deep compassion

- I now rise from the depths

# Chapter 2 –

# Stand True

# Beside Mother

Dare to love yourself as if you were a
rainbow with gold at both ends.


Aberjhani

*As women, our relationship with our Mothers can be one of the most influential relationships of our lifetime. Our personal relationship with our Mother influences our perspective on what it is to be a woman, whether we feel we can trust other women and on being Mothers ourselves. Irrespective of how loving and nurturing our Mothers were or were not in our lives, we all reach our adult years with unmet emotional needs. No earthly woman has the capacity to show up and meet all of her child's emotional needs. While we all hope that those blessed to become Mothers will honour their children with the very best care and devotion they can bring, the truth is that at some moment every Mother will find herself incapable of meeting the needs of her child.*

A s Daughters, we each have our own experience of having our needs met to varying degrees. While it may be tempting to step into a position of blame for gaps when our own Mothers did not offer what we sought, I believe it's our sacred opportunity to find how we can self-mother. Through self-mothering, we can each learn how to perceive our own unmet needs and find the willingness and commitment to offer this to ourselves – and to accept this gift.

Stephanie held a powerful presence: her wisdom was practically palpable. I could sense she knew the road of loss and that she had come a huge distance on her path of ascension. On the first day we met, she relayed a story about how as a 5 year old she had been convinced that home was not a safe place. Concerned for her sister's safety, she packed only the essentials and with her beloved sister's hand in hers, set off for brighter horizons. This woman was brave as a child and could see the inability within her Mother to meet the physical and emotional needs of herself and - more importantly - her sister. Their escape lasted only briefly before being brought home, where it would be some considerable time before she could again find her way out of her family home and onto the path of her liberation and independence.

Stephanie was adamant that she could find her own way in this harsh world. With noble intentions she set off, but unfortunately found little opportunity or support as a young 16 year old. With a mountain of unmet emotional needs, Stephanie's heart ached to be loved, known, cherished and cared for. It wasn't long before her search to fulfil these needs was met with a series of promiscuous liaisons. Seeking to fulfil the secret longing of her heart in the arms of men became a flurry of deep dives that only left her coming up thirstier than before.

It would take some years of seeking love in the arms of men to confirm that there was no pure water available to truly satisfy the thirst within. The experience of each new encounter brought Stephanie a depth of insight that enriched her wisdom. Many would turn to Stephanie to seek guidance on their path and her wisdom proved potent and powerful every time.

Eventually Stephanie could see that she needed to return to where her journey had begun – her relationship with her Mother. With a strike of powerful inspiration, Stephanie knew it was time to express for herself what had never been permitted in her home - a declaration of the truth. With fervent conviction and an honourable depth of courage, Stephanie allowed herself to pour out a love letter addressed straight to her mum. It relayed the details of secret moments that her Mother had no knowledge of. It expressed the disappointment and sadness of a little girl who felt she couldn't turn to her Mother or even feel safe in her presence. Stephanie allowed herself to detail experiences occurring in her youth which she didn't know whether her Mother knew about or not. For the first time, she told her Mum the truth of what had happened. In a family in which open discussions were non-existent, Stephanie knew she needed to air out her soul. She trusted herself to open her heart to the one woman she had hoped could have been there to guide her and nurture her through those early formative years.

With conviction, the letter was in the post and Stephanie didn't know what outcome would tumble forward from her committed action. After a passage of time, Stephanie received a letter in the mail box from her own Mother, who had written back in reply. Her investment of honesty, trust and open-hearted sharing had moved her Mother and permitted her to also share in the sacred expression of her own feelings and experiences. Hearing from her own Mother and witnessing the precious and harrowing details from her own life confirmed what Stephanie had guessed was true, but had not been confirmed until now. Stephanie breathed in all of her Mother's sacred sharing and witnessed how her own pain had only been a repeat of the pain her Mother had first encountered.

These women gave each other permission to be seen, as they revealed themselves. Both of them felt a wash of deep compassion, comprehending how unified they both were in many of their past undesirable circumstances. Stephanie's mum revealed her own personal pain, resulting from being sexually abused by close family members. Ashamed of what had happened, she had kept silent for fear of judgment. Standing together naked they both felt more clothed in truth than the pair could have imagined possible. A newfound mutual respect and compassion engulfed their relationship as each woman felt acknowledged, forgiven and held in compassionate love.

Stephanie could feel the ramifications of her brave extension as it rippled out over her life, allowing her to feel more connected within, more seen and deeply embraced. Now she had the light and conviction to usher in the next level of healing for herself. Her relationships with men had been fraught with peril; they were all started in hope, yet proved unfulfilling. Stephanie had been unknowingly seeking love from the opposite sex. Our thirst for the love we felt wasn't present early on in life can blind us, as we compulsively seek it outside of ourselves.

Stephanie had joined me for a live event, seeking the truth she required to heal this shadow pattern which was puppeteering her romantic life. With breathtaking clarity, Stephanie was shown that the source of love emanated from within her; she saw the rich supply that the heavens glowed down through her crown chakra and recognised that all that was left was for her to give herself permission to receive it. Yes, she knew it was true. The journey of seeking had ended with her great heart finding. She willingly brought forward full permission for herself to receive and bask in this divine love daily.

While we all have different degrees of unmet needs, any unmet need will still beg to be fulfilled. In our grief, the path to receive the love we seek can be fraught with gatekeepers who request a portion of our truth while promising our wishes will be fulfilled. In the pain of giving our power away and still finding love lacking, we become awakened to seek a source of true love that can receive us as we are and replenish us fully.

We each receive the sacred privilege of learning how to self-mother and permit ourselves to receive from the heavens what we require. Becoming lost in the myriad of counterfeit forms of love only serves to clarify the true source. As we become honest and truthful within ourselves, we are led home to bask in an infinite supply of heavenly love.

# *Healing Guidance*

1. What emotional needs are seeking fulfilment within you now?
   *(i.e. to be heard, acknowledged, witnessed? To receive tenderness, caring, quality time, affirmation, gentle touch, nurture, or reassurance?)*

2. What is the one most powerful way you could self-mother yourself today?

3. What self care routines does your heart require in your life right now?
   *(i.e. daily journaling, exercise, meditation, acts of kindness, having a bath, listening to music, painting, writing, spending time in nature, lighting a candle, going to bed early, reading a good book etc.)*

## Visualisation:

*To bring loving awareness to your relationship with your Mother, allow yourself to see her standing before you. Allow yourself to visualise your Mother in her truth, and breathe in the truth of what your heart needs to remember right now.*

| *Wounded perspective* | *Healed perspective* |
|---|---|
| **My Mother doesn't love me** | **The Divine Mother holds me in her grace, love and compassion** |
| **I'm unlovable** | **I am love** |
| **I don't deserve love** | **Infinite love cocoons me** |

# Healing Affirmations

- Love is all there is

- I allow myself to sit here now

- Truth brings me peace

- I see how loved I truly am

- Even in my loss, I was held in love

# Chapter 3 -

# Stand True

# Beside Father

Shine

like the whole

universe

is yours


Rumi

*Having a genuine desire for approval, acceptance and recognition from our Father is as natural as squinting our eyes while walking in heavy rain. While it's natural to seek this love, there are Fathers who can't or won't love us in the way we yearn for. Generational wounding means that our Fathers have often suffered neglect or abuse in a way that affects their capacity to show up in the deeply admiring and accepting way that would be ideal. While their withheld approval can become our first experiences of rejection, it turns out their way of loving has little to do with who we are.*

Our path is to ascend the circumstances we find ourselves in and turn the predicaments of our lives into the reasons why we rise. Elaine was the daughter of an actor, and it just so happened that she too had an unquenchable thirst for acting. Her skill and passion for performance was evident from an early age as well as her Father's disapproval of her body shape and size. He implied that 'being a successful actress would require a slim, hourglass figure' and Elaine's Father had concerns that his daughter may not have a chance of success in this career due to his perception of her current physique.

Rarely discussed openly, Elaine's weight was included in a level of conversational exchange that was not overt and yet felt unceasingly present. Feeling unacceptable in her body and unsupported in her dreams became a theme that would span decades.

Despite the subtle discouragement and hints at how her weight could affect her potential acting career, Elaine strode on and became deeply devoted to her dreams, despite the discouragement she felt. When Elaine and I were brought together, we felt an instant kinship. I could perceive the depth of pain that Elaine held within. Few knew of the internal torment she faced daily. She placed all of her creative energy into developing her career, while internally battling the idea that her body shape would destine her to failure.

Elaine knew the depth of tenderness within the human heart. She found within herself a great love for people and the precious stories of their lives. She was a powerful listener - always willing to hear, offer encouragement and convey hope that if the desire existed, then the path to fulfil that yearning must also be present. She was well known for her wisdom and had gathered a delicious assortment of friends and colleagues who respected and admired her art of living.

Despite the negative presumption that Elaine's acting career would be limited by her size, the opposite was in fact proven repeatedly. Elaine was able to shine when performing and truly embody characters with a depth of richness and authenticity that allowed the story to be witnessed and swiftly absorbed by an enchanted audience. On stage, being able to embody different characters allowed Elaine to escape the terrain of her own soul and step into new emotional landscapes that were highly preferable. Together, we both gave Elaine permission to travel within and face the state of her relationship with her Father. Interestingly, it's these painful triggers from our past that forge our unique purpose. Elaine was devoted to pursuing her career despite her appearance and developed a deep commitment to offer acceptance and compassion to everyone who crossed her path. Would she have been this dedicated to offering love had she not felt so unsupported in her relationship with her own Father, earlier in life?

Giving space and time for painful threads of our past to unravel and unknot takes courage and submission. I felt prompted to ask Elaine how she could honour and appreciate her Father for what he had withheld from her. The tears flowed and the pain surfaced. Elaine was able to see how her own Father's pain had prevented him from accepting and admiring his own precious daughter and the career she had forged in his shadow. A natural willingness sprang forward to forgive her dad, and along with that a generous supply of acceptance and approval for herself. The ache dissipated as Elaine retrieved her power and stood firmly in a new commitment to remove 'judgement' from her relationship with herself and to pursue her career from a place of self-compassion and deep self acceptance.

Months later, Elaine informed me of an up-coming surgery. She had felt inspired to have her gastric lat-band removed so she could step firmly into self love. I had no idea that over a decade ago, Elaine had felt so deeply concerned for her weight and its affect on her whole life (let alone her career), that she had resorted to a secret surgery to amend the problem. The lat-band had brought changes to her weight, and yet it brought a flurry of complications to her eating and relationship with food and herself. None of her friends knew that physical complications from the lat-band were affecting Elaine's life. Once she shared the surgery date with me, I invited her to open her heart and share the news with some of her closest friends. You see, keeping her suffering a secret was preventing Elaine from seeing the enormous love and support that so many of her friends have for her. Reluctant and scared of judgment, Elaine confided in a dear friend about the upcoming surgery and its cause. Upon hearing the news, this dear friend threw her arms around Elaine and hugged her in a wave of deep love that Elaine had rarely allowed herself to receive.

Elaine was beginning to witness how freeing truth is and how speaking the truth of her situation could bring judgement or it could bring love, acceptance and compassion. Elaine committed to bring a new level of honesty to all of her relationships, allowing herself to not only love deeply as she always did, but learn how to gently open to receive love, acceptance and support from others.

I recently heard from Elaine after another series of successful shows. The resonance in her voice was clear, confirming her confidence in and appreciation of her rising career. Then she continued to relay how she had not only delivered a soul tingling performance that brought a standing ovation, but for the first time she actually allowed herself to open the breadth of her own heart and breathe in the appreciation. Allowing this form of love within her soul was powerfully healing for Elaine as she conditioned herself to allow love, acceptance and support to flow into her life and fill an area she had given up knowing could ever be touched.

The pain that Elaine had encountered in her relationship with her Father felt like a sharp thorn that couldn't be removed. As soon as Elaine allowed herself to perceive the enormous pain within her Father's heart, she was able to set his opinions and behaviour aside and choose to receive from herself and others the love, approval and acceptance that she had always longed for. Realising that she had given up on ever receiving support and encouragement meant that Elaine had buried her natural desire to receive it. She buried it down so deeply, she could almost imagine it wasn't there. But the things which ache within us are calling for our loving awareness.

Learning how to speak her truth, and allow herself to receive this powerful love, brought in waves of relief and restoration that gave Elaine new life. Giving to ourselves that which has been in little or no supply allows us to rise from our descent and embody our divine purpose in a way that truly touches the souls of everyone in our reach.

# Healing Guidance

1. Name the one thing you wish your Dad was able to offer you more of in your youth.

2. What is the most powerful lesson that your Dad has provided you with over his lifetime?

3. What level of safety and security do you have in your life right now? (10 is a sense of total conceivable safety and security and 0 is no safety or security.)

## Visualisation:

*To bring loving awareness to your relationship with your Father, allow yourself to see him standing before you. Allow yourself to visualise your Father in his truth, and breathe in the truth of what your heart needs to remember right now.*

| *Wounded perspective* | *Healed perspective* |
|---|---|
| **My Father** <br> **never approved** | **My Heavenly Father** <br> **adores me** |
| **I'm a failure** | **I can create any desire** <br> **with love** |
| **Men can't love me** | **Universal love flows** <br> **through me** |

# Healing Affirmations

- Infinite love is available to me

- I forgive my Father for what he couldn't provide

- I forgive myself for holding myself down

- I give myself permission to shine my light

- I acknowledge my anger and bathe myself in love

# Chapter 4 -

# Stand True

# Beside

# Siblings

My soul honours your soul.
I honour the love, light, beauty, truth
and kindness within you, because it is also
within me.

In sharing these things, there is no
distance and no difference between us.
We are the same. We are one.

Author unknown

*Our siblings come forward through the same heritage line of love, and while so much of who we are is shared, our unique differences can provide dramatic contrast. Where rich connection lies, heart ties can pull tight. Sharing the same upbringing can bond siblings together, yet the nuances of personality can tear that connection apart. Seeking to receive the love we crave from a sibling is as catastrophic as attempting to be the love your sibling seeks.*

Naomi was a first born; she had a few years with her parents before Samantha was born. Naomi adored her beautiful baby sister, and the four of them grew together. Naomi was incredibly perceptive of her parents' wounds. Being a highly sensitive empath meant that in her presence, the emotional pain from their past would surface. Her parents reacted to their daughter's innate gift and called her names, due to the reaction they believed she 'caused' within them. Naomi was actually just a born healer who loved declaring truth. Her parents had little reprieve as their shadow tendencies were identified and revealed by their passionate eldest daughter. While Naomi was confident, creative and known for standing her ground, Samantha was more reserved, cautious and sensitive.

As children, they spent thousands of hours playing, talking and adoring one another. The girls had such deep love for one another and yet each secretly yearned for the characteristics they saw shining in their sibling. Naomi noticed Samantha's timidity and observed how it brought her more sensitive responses and gentle affection. Samantha admired her big sister's courage and confidence. She was aware of how popular her sister was among her friends. Naomi was always so clear in the way she could express herself. However, neither sister would dare breathe mention of the secret longing they both held to emulate one another.

Both girls perceived a lack of love and saw one another as the responsible culprit; thus a secret rivalry was born. Play dates in the kitchen and games in the park would reveal two beautiful sisters who loved one another dearly, but their innate differences left them both feeling pegged against one another. As one sister would shine in her element, the other would shrink back and desperately fear that her contrast would disqualify her from the love she sought from their parents and everyone else connected to their lives.

Small experiences mounted up over time and the sisters' rivalry became entrenched in their hearts; they could only perceive their own lack in one another's presence. As they became older, their friendship circles changed and the continual comparison seemed to abate for a time until Naomi got engaged. Jealousy reared up as Samantha began to feel insignificant in light of Naomi's upcoming wedding.

I met Naomi at a live event a few years after her wedding when her first child had just become a toddler. Naomi felt raw and unsettled within herself. Tired, misunderstood and exhausted, she was the shell of who she once was. Naomi found solace in our work together, as she carved out time and space to support herself to understand her emotional world and digest some of the big experiences that life had brought her. She longed to find a sense of connection with herself, her own life and was desperate to create the family harmony she had never known.

Naomi spoke of Samantha with a depth of fondness that I had rarely observed. Such rich admiration for her sister covered a painful pattern of competing for love. They had both been locked in a match vying for supremacy in the hope of receiving their parents' approval.

Supporting Naomi to understand her role in this push-pull competitive relationship progressed gently. Naomi recalled how they would even vie for attention with competitive illnesses. If Naomi had a migraine, Samantha would have a tummy ache, to ensure the attention would return to her. There were so many ways that this pattern played out, and as Naomi shone in her truth, it would infuriate her sister. Naomi began to see how she dimmed her light in an attempt to prevent her sister's jealousy. She also recognised how she and her sister had become locked in a battle of comparative strengths and weaknesses for so long that they had become disconnected from the unique power and purpose they each held.

Naomi had willingly packed away her truth, in the hope that she wouldn't ruffle her sister's feathers. And while this had never been successful, Naomi placated herself, believing that watering herself down definitely helped to minimise the damage in her sister's life. There had been so much turning off within herself to avoid activating her sister's jealousy that Naomi was now left facing all of the closed doors within her own soul. Naomi began to see how she gave up her power and surrendered her truth to placate and support a sister who was lost in her own pain and perspective of inadequacy. I encouraged Naomi to find ways to hold Samantha in love, so she could be herself and not bow to her sister's insecurities any longer. Helping Naomi to see that others don't need to be wrong in order for us to be right shifted the relationship dynamic instantly. Seeing how they could both be true to who they were and also be loved brought a wash of relief to Naomi's heart.

Naomi began owning her intuitive connection and began allowing her inner knowing to lead her life. Naomi fell within and began throwing open all the doors inside herself so she could discover the freedom of true authentic expression once more. She also beamed so much love into her dear sister's life that she knew within herself that her own shining couldn't detract from the power and validity of Samantha's own bright light.

We all seek love and when we try to find love in our families at the expense of our siblings, we cut ourselves off from source.

Our unique attributes are essential for our path, and while we all differ, the glory we each gain from shining in our own power is the same. If you feel that a sibling or anyone is intimidated by you, send them deep love and continue to shine bright. When we give ourselves permission to step deeply into the truth and potency of who we are, we will activate others around us who have yet to own their own light. Nevertheless, standing in our power is a gift we give ourselves and the biggest permission slip we can produce, to help others see that they too can find the safety, magnificence and power of living true to their own divine purpose.

# Healing Guidance

1. Name the sibling or cousin that you were most jealous of when growing up.

2. Reflect on how you are both different from each other.

3. Ask yourself, "Am I ready to forgive myself?" for giving my power away to my sibling/cousin?

## Visualisation:

*To bring loving awareness to your sibling or cousin, allow yourself to see him/her standing before you. Allow yourself to visualise your sibling or cousin in his/her truth, and breathe in the truth of what your heart needs to remember right now.*

| *Wounded perspective* | *Healed perspective* |
| --- | --- |
| I'm not good enough | I am perfect in my truth |
| I don't fit in | I shine in my uniqueness |
| I don't belong | I'm exactly where I need to be right now |

# Healing Affirmations

- I forgive myself

- I hold my sibling/cousin in love

- I allow myself to shine in my truth

- I hold myself in love

- I bring compassion to the past

# Chapter 5 –

# Stand True

# Beside

# Friends

*You, yourself, as much as anybody in the entire universe, deserves your love and affection.*

*Buddah*

*In order for us to learn how to transcend and stand in the glory of our truth and purpose, we must first give away all of our power. Those drawn to this book are at the point of ascension, as you have already faced and survived your loss and grief. After being bewildered, detached and hopeless for a time, the light is kindled within to comprehend our united human experience of suffering – that no one is exempt. In this awareness we begin to recognise how others around us now are currently experiencing what we once believed would destroy us. I honour my suffering for its loving call to humility; in owning my own powerlessness I was able to open to a power far greater than I knew was available. It is only by relying on this light and the many promptings it nudges us forward with, that over time we are brought to a place where we find the very means to conquer what once befell us. Our appreciation for the depth of this pain truly does activate our enormous capacity to give.*

No matter how much love and support we did or didn't receive in our formative early years, we all come out of our childhood with unmet needs. These unmet needs begin to develop, and refine us, and cultivate our gifts, from very early on in our lives. The specific ways in which you did not receive the love that you yearned for provided a particularly powerful insight into the hurt and sense of disconnection that is born when we don't receive what we crave. We attract individuals into our lives that act as a reflection of who we once were and when we meet this reflection, we feel inclined and drawn to sharing and imparting with them that which we never knew.

Being willing to give what *we* didn't receive activates our nobility, as we see the growth and healing revealed when we give what we did not know. In doing so, we discover the power of finding how to securely invest it within our own hearts as well.

Louisa is a powerful example of how we can give our power away seeking love, acceptance and validation from friends. I met Louisa and was instantly impressed by her beauty, confidence and charisma. Beneath her gorgeous exterior lay a mountain of vulnerable neediness; within, she was seeking, pleading and hiding her need for approval and acceptance. Appearances are definitely deceiving and while Louisa could strike up a conversation with anyone, she secretly wished someone could reassure her and confirm that she was likable, lovable and worth being friends with.

It was Louisa's relationship with her husband which drew her to work with me. Challenges in her marriage and intimate life were becoming unbearable and it was time to look within and heal, or walk away to potentially recreate the same experience again. Louisa has a strong connection with her intuition, and while she couldn't see what was causing the disparate separateness in her marriage, she was committed to healing herself from within.

Taking gigantic leaps into vulnerability and with piercing honesty, Louisa confided how desperately she wanted to be wanted. The fire and appeal her husband had held for her had now diminished, after years of marriage and giving birth to their first child. Afraid to ask for intimacy for fear of being rejected, Louisa became blocked from drawing close to her husband, and he had now begun reflecting back her inability to ask for what he wanted – intimacy was at a standstill.

Tension mounted, a sense of separateness developed and Louisa's fear that she was unwanted felt validated; an old ache became increasingly apparent, intensifying with current conditions. Together we set a powerful intention to bring healing to this invisible wound, trusting that together we would be led to its source. Very quickly, Louisa recalled an experience from her younger life, involving a friend named Alarna who lived on the same street; they would walk to school together and play together often, sharing their neighbouring childhood homes.

Surprisingly, one year Louisa was not invited to Alarna's birthday party and the realisation that Alarna for some reason no longer liked her was mortifying. Alarna began showing Louisa how much she now disliked her and the taunting began: teasing Louisa with cruel names, literally and emotionally throwing stones at her on the walk home from school in a powerful display of non-love. The sense of betrayal and shock of rejection took Louisa's breath away; she simply couldn't comprehend how she could be treated like this after having such a close friendship with Alarna until just recently. The taunting increased and walking home from school became a sullen, fearful and confusing experience for Louisa, who constantly wondered what she had done wrong. Why was she no longer good enough for Alarna? Louisa was desperate to comprehend what she could do to once again be found worthy and be liked.

From this young age, Louisa secretly hid her fear that she would not be liked. She persistently sought out friends who would like her and would confirm they wanted to be friends with her, but in going to great lengths to win approval, Louisa was left feeling exhausted, fearful and busy. Trying to be 'liked' by a myriad of difference people is impossible, but Louisa's heartache re-emerged whenever she perceived anyone disapproving or disliking her. This perpetuated the cycle of trying to be more likable, lovable and wanted again!

Fast forward decades and the secret self-belief that she wasn't lovable meant that Louisa had developed, refined and cultivated herself to be an inspiring and encouraging person who appreciated and accepted all of her friends. Louisa was liked by many because of her capacity to like, want and care for her own friends. She could give the love that she wasn't shown, but it still wasn't enough to validate her secret fear that she was not worth befriending herself.

The wound of being unwanted remained close to the surface, and working so hard to be likeable had ensured her a degree of un-rejectability that, for the most part, placated her. Nevertheless, the shadow side of this compensating behaviour reared its head in her marriage. Working so hard to be socially likeable with women and female friends meant there was little left to invest in her relationship. Coming home, Louisa looked to her husband to show her how wanted, desirable and lovable she was, but his efforts simply didn't suffice. While she craved his attention, she unknowingly pushed his love away.

In the shock of Alarna's cruel and unexpected behaviour, Louisa realised that she had given her power away; she began deceiving herself to believe that she must somehow augment herself to become sufficient and worthy of the friendship she craved. Finding this gold was a harrowing moment of ascension; in refusing to give Alarna the power to 'define' her worth, Louisa was free to bask in the heaven-revealed truth of her perfection, value and infinite worth. Realising that she actually need do nothing to be worthy of love and friendship, Louisa gave herself permission to accept the kindness and care she had showered upon so many others, to now reinvest securely within her own sacred heart.

Shoulders rested and squared, heart safe now in love, Louisa was free to bask in her new knowing and saw it shift her relationship with her friends, daughter and husband. Giving herself what she had not received - acceptance, approval and friendship - meant that Louisa had a new-found power and potency. She no longer looked to her husband to fill an invisible gap, she was free to show up and share her bountiful abundance of love with her husband and freely receive the same in return.

# Healing Guidance

1. Name one friend you felt betrayed by when you were younger?

2. What were you looking for in that friendship that you can now give to yourself?

3. Write down three ways in which you can be a better friend to yourself in order to strengthen your current good friendships and attract more?

## Visualisation:

*To bring loving awareness to your friend, allow yourself to see him/her standing before you. Allow yourself to visualise your friend in his/her truth, and breathe in the truth of what your heart needs to remember right now.*

| Wounded perspective | Healed perspective |
| --- | --- |
| I've been betrayed | I forgive those who hurt me |
| I can't trust anyone | I can trust myself |
| I need them to like me | I deeply and completely love and accept myself |

# Healing Affirmations

- I am taught by many teachers

- I breathe in love

- I breathe out forgiveness

- I hold myself in deep compassion

- I stand by myself at all times

# Chapter 6 -

# Feel Guided

# LYSA BLACK

If you knew who walked beside you at all times, on the path that you have chosen, you could never experience fear or doubt again.

Wayne Dyer

*When we truly feel that our light has been extinguished, it marks the precise moment when loving energies enter to sprinkle our souls with new life and show us that we are not alone. Hope for a possible future heaven is transformed by a knowing that heaven surrounds us now.*

Our weak cries to angels become clear two-way conversations and our hopeless prayers become a deep sense of trust in the feelings we can now sense are present within. Heavenly guidance is right inside our own beating chest, and a knowing that we are held, loved and guided always resounds.

Melinda joined in a live webinar online with me and witnessed the most amazing vision of an angel close by her. For the longest time Melinda had thought she was alone in her challenges and while she hoped her prayers were heard, any sign of a positive response was unrecognisable.

Drawn to working together, Melinda began opening her heart to me and sharing the depth of grief that she had been carrying for 14 years. Her husband struggled with mental illness and while he was an intelligent loving Father and husband, he had taken his own life and left behind their two young children for Melinda to raise all on her own. The financial strain of his departure had massive ramifications for his grieving widow. She lost her home, her sense of security and belief in the heavens.

Now, 14 years later, Melinda could feel a stirring within herself, a kind of awakening in which she was beginning to see, sense and feel the guidance of spirit in her life. Confirming messages from close friends, visiting animals bearing whispers of sacred guidance, and nudges within to be still, began to flow into every day of Melinda's life.

Our healing sessions together gave Melinda permission to reflect on her loss in a way that was safe. She could finally feel she was held in love as she reflected. Realising that she had never permitted herself to grieve - instead focusing on simply surviving every day - had left Melinda disconnected, tired and exhausted. The weariness of her deep grief had etched itself on her bones and was beginning to slow Melinda down.

Learning how to turn to her divine mother and feel a sense of being held, nurtured and loved was an experience which turned the tide in Melinda's weary soul. With so many years spent in devotion to two Fatherless children and the need to provide financially, Melinda was exhausted. As soon as she allowed her inner little girl to be held, she felt the sprinkling of the waters of life and began to feel restored. The combination of being devoted in service to her **children and** her professional role as a nurse had left Melinda devoid of any capacity to nurture her own soul, but now, as she felt her little self held and embraced, her breath deepened and life returned.

Melinda became fascinated by the nudges, whispers and sense of connection that was awakening in her life. Finally she could sense the guidance being whispered and it opened her eyes to a new world. There was still a heavy weight, which hung from her frame every day – her care and devotion to her two children were the fundamental element of Melinda's existence, but worrying about, serving and caring for them felt like an overwhelming daily burden. As it grew heavier, the weariness and tiresome sense of responsibility towards her two dear children began taking more than she had to offer. Despite their maturing near adult ages, Melinda's dedication to their care seemed impossible to adjust.

Together we sought clarity and I asked if she had experienced loss before her husband's passing? "No, I haven't lost anyone" she replied and the conversation carried on for some minutes, even shifting to a new topic, when suddenly Melinda shared; "Wait... I miscarried 3 babies before I had my children" and as the knowing flowed into her mind, it brought a torrent of tears and sadness. We both cried together.

Melinda chose to bury her grief along with her children, who had known so little of life. She had forgotten this great loss and instead of mourning what had not been permitted to be, she had held onto her living children with her whole soul. She carried and held her children in a way that would ensure she could never lose any of her babies again... or so she thought! The weight of worry and attempt to carry them as adults emotionally, spiritually and mentally had taken a toll and exhausted this well meaning mother.

Being able to acknowledge her loss brought a wave of understanding and relief. Her innate response to carry her living children beyond the normal expectations of mothering suddenly made complete sense; the knee-jerk reaction to 'hold' her children after losing her babies was an unconscious act that had remained hidden for 14 years.

Finding relief, healing and truth transformed Melinda's perception of loving guidance. Her sense of knowing that spirit was leading her became a deep knowing that imbued strength, life and light into Melinda's being – transforming her inner world.

We all fear our time finishing before we are ready to leave. Each of us has a secret knowing within that we are all here for a particular mission, purpose, life or destiny that no other can fulfil. Melinda worked in the field of healthcare and discovered that her depth of loss gave her the ability to truly devote herself in service to these precious souls. Her exposure to losing some of those closest to her taught her the value of perceiving the soul within the body before their eventual passing over. Melinda had a way of reaching the soul through her loving perception that granted aged individuals the chance to truly feel seen, loved and cared for.

Just as we fall screaming into an abyss of darkness, the fall bottoms out to a skyline of light and, floating still, we realise that we are held in grace and received in love. We see that having our light extinguished is just the moment before our new birth begins. From this side we gain a fearless devotion to our divine purpose, a grateful reliance on spiritual guidance and a commitment to use our suffering to bless others.

The descent reaches its most bitter nadir as our light is extinguished. Moments later we rise, realigned with a new path of ascension that fails to recede. This resurrection, awakening or moment of grace is inevitable and marks the pivotal point of triumph as we shift into our power, truth and divine purpose.

Melinda represents the depth of grief that we have all known, we all comprehend the requirements of daily life and how they can require us to function today, preventing us from ever finding the space to mourn, acknowledge and grieve for what we have lost.

# Healing Guidance

1. Is it time to grieve what you have lost? Dedicating time, space and honesty to grieve our hardships can give our hearts space to awaken to the guidance available to us.

2. What responsibilities are you carrying in order to avoid being with your own inner world?

3. Have you been making yourself too busy to sit and allow yourself to connect with the messages and whispers wanting to guide and bless you?

## Visualisation:

*To bring loving awareness to the third eye, allow yourself to see deep inky dark blue, swirling beautifully around your third eye (the area between your eyebrows).*

| Wounded perspective | Healed perspective |
| --- | --- |
| I do not know what to believe | I see the truth |
| There has been a big mistake | I see perfection |
| Nothing makes sense | I see divine love |

# Healing Affirmations

- I trust myself to see the truth

- I allow myself to sit here now

- Truth brings me peace

- I see how loved I truly am

- Even in my loss, I was held in love

# Chapter 7 - Speak Truth

*Truth*

*is the only*

*safe ground*

*to stand*

*upon.*

Elizabeth Cady Stanton

*Learning to be quiet and withhold the truth can be an act of preserving dignity and avoiding conflict. When our circumstances don't support the declaration of truth, we all have the ability to become quiet and choose to keep our wisdom, truth and opinions to ourselves. While we remain quiet, we are saved from outer discontent but begin creating inner discontent. Withholding our truth may save others from discomfort, but it disempowers us from being able to create the change we were born to usher in.*

Our throat chakra is our voice, our capacity to speak our truth. It's the power centre from which we declare who we are, what we think and how we plan to action our intentions.

We will all encounter many gate-keepers who will ask us to be quiet. Some of them will be close to us and some will simply be passing through our lives briefly. We will all develop the capacity to comply, to be quiet and keep our truth unseen and unheard from the world in an act of self-protection - you cannot be criticised for an opinion if it remains unheard and unknown.

Once we choose to see our secrecy and withholding as being a valuable way to avoid criticism, attack, conflict and challenge, we begin descending. The longer we withhold our truth, the further we will descend into powerlessness – even to a point where we may not feel safe to share any portion of who we are and what we truly think with anyone, including ourselves.

Feeling helpless, powerless and invisible to this degree initiates our eventual spiritual death. We can reach a point where all of our light fades and we continue to move around as a shell, devoid of feeling and light. Being led to remember the value of our voice, the inherent wisdom in our perspective and the power of speaking our heart and mind brings a sense of liberation and purpose that raises us and our quality of life to a new high. We cannot align with our divine purpose without our ability to speak truth.

Belinda was a soft and tender woman who was deeply sensitive. She was raised in a large family with a devoted Father and Mother who believed in unity, quality time and harmony. While the temporal needs were provided in this family, emotional needs were invalid and unrecognised as the material necessities took precedence. The emphasis on unity required strict discipline, to ensure that all four children got along and harmony reigned.

Belinda loved time with her family, but she always yearned to engage with activities that differed from their interests. In this family, if one child played soccer, they all played soccer! Individual needs were less important than ensuring they all participated in one activity together. Belinda had desires to try things outside of the family status quo, but any requests were swiftly dismissed with raised voices. Belinda therefore learnt over the years to stop asking for what she wanted and to stop sharing her opinion, in order to keep the peace. But in doing so, hopelessness was born; a fear within Belinda that her desires and opinions were invalid. Any hope that she could do the things she yearned to do was extinguished. In order to cope with the rigours of this environment, Belinda not only became quiet and reserved, never sharing her thoughts, opinions or desires, but in time she actually forgot that they were even there.

By the time she was married, Belinda was completely unsure about what she wanted for her career at all. There seemed to be a void within; circumstances had required her to ignore these parts of herself to the point where it felt like they had actually vanished. Belinda was highly intelligent and capable of doing many things, but without being able to connect to a sense of desire, passion and intention she was continually disappointed and frustrated with herself for being so unclear about her career direction.

After coming to me because her own attempts to find her

passion were fruitless, apathy was seeping in and dragging all of the blessings of her life down. Belinda's health and family life were lacklustre and her loving husband was at a loss to help, because she didn't know how to find an occupation that lit her up.

When questioned around what she wanted, silence was the usual response; she simply couldn't connect with anything within herself. The more Belinda shared about her up-bringing, the more it became clear what the actual barrier was. Through our work together, Belinda realised that she wanted to find a way to speak up for herself with her family in a way that respected them but still honoured her.

An important family event was organised that didn't fit with Belinda's schedule, and the angst around her potentially 'not attending' was obvious. She had been instructed for half a lifetime to go with her parents' plan for their family and put her own needs, wants and desires aside. Belinda was able to see how she had been conditioned to give her power away to her parents and simply do whatever they asked. Anger came rising to the surface as Belinda found a sense of resoluteness that she was no longer going to play along with the family status quo; she knew she had to prioritise her own family and her own life.

As a result of this realisation, Belinda plucked up the courage to tell her family that she wasn't attending the family event and that her decision was final. Her decision caused massive waves across her whole family and Belinda hated the discontent she felt she was creating, but somehow she knew that standing firm was an important commitment to herself. Belinda felt uncomfortable observing how her family reacted, but she also felt a new sense of relief and liberation that for the first time in her adult life she had spoken up! In saying 'No', Belinda established the power to say what she wanted in her life. She had found the means to give herself what she wanted.

Within six months Belinda had radically changed her relationship with her family; while she loved them dearly, she gave herself permission to reply honestly about whether or not she wanted to be involved in their plans. Sometimes she said no and stayed away, other times she connected with them and felt more joy than ever, knowing it was her choice to be in their company. She simultaneously began speaking up more in her workplace. Sharing her ideas and perspectives created new-found respect from her team and manager, but the real transformation took place within Belinda. By taking a big risk to speak up for herself, Belinda opened herself back up to her own inner world, which had once felt like a void but was now swarming with desires, passions, interests and plans that she was learning how to acknowledge and act upon for the first time in her adult life.

Fast forward another year and Belinda had actually realised how essential it was for her to be living in deep devotion to her own family. She left her employment to invest herself completely in supporting her husband, his work, and seeing her own family flourish in the unique ways they each desired. Seeing how each of them were free and supported to be true to themselves gave Belinda the greatest sense of joy she had ever known.

Speaking our truth isn't merely about expressing our opinions; our voice also reflects our power, our perspective, our wishes, our desires and our boundaries. Holding ourselves in love while we deepen into giving ourselves full permission to speak the truth of who we are and what we desire reconnects us with a sense of power and capacity to fulfil ourselves. Belinda bravely took her power back, learnt to speak up with her family and was able to reconnect with her sacred inner world of desires and dreams.

# Healing Guidance

1. Have you been quiet for too long? Reflect on the different areas of your life and acknowledge where you are speaking your truth, and where you want to start sharing more? (i.e. Relationship, Parenting, Finances, Employment, Business, Extended Family, Social Media)

2. What's the one thing you know it's time to tell someone important?

3. Are you ready to confide in yourself? If you are not ready to speak your truth with anyone else yet, give yourself permission to pour out a 'Truth Letter' to yourself. Begin by writing: "The truth is…"

## Visualisation:

*To bring loving awareness to the throat chakra, allow yourself to see a vibrant ocean blue swirling beautifully around your lower throat area.*

| *Wounded perspective* | *Healed perspective* |
|---|---|
| **No one will believe me** | **I speak my truth** |
| **I'm not allowed to share** | **I express myself** |
| **I cannot speak** | **I speak clearly** |

# Healing Affirmations

- I speak up for myself

- I share my true feelings

- I know what's right for me

- I share my true thoughts

- My truth is heard and received

# Chapter 8 -

# Reciprocate

# Love

What you

vibrate out

into your world,

the universe

echoes back.


*Panache Desai*

*Love, in its finest and highest expression on earth, is an experience of reciprocation. It's when two hearts freely share, connect and raise each other up. I've noticed there's a view that giving love is a higher, more worthy act, while receiving or sharing in love is less noble. However, when we are solely in the act of giving love, we can attract the 'takers' or 'receivers' of love. Powerful ripples of true love emanate when two hearts connect and vibrate in mutual devotion and reciprocation. Mother/Daughter relationships in which both are held in mutual respect and honour, thrive with a powerful sense of fulfilment and joy. Father/Son relationships involving mutual deep respect and high esteem, rise higher together. Husbands and wives who do this, siblings who do this, and friends who do this all know the power of being devoted to mutual honour and respect; the true reciprocation of exalting love.*

L ilah was a lover. She cared deeply for others. As a natural healer, she was remarkable at nurturing with her highly sensitive empathic gift. Her heart was incredibly discerning of emotional needs and she naturally found herself lifting and loving those around her. A conversation with Lilah was a sure way for others to walk away feeling supported and reassured.

But when Lilah came to me, her gift was out of balance. Her great capacity to love was limited by an inability to know how to love herself and allow herself to be loved. While she was easily aware of the true emotional state of others, she was often disconnected and out of touch with how she really felt. She would go to great lengths to care for others, but gave little time and attention to herself.

She regularly used her spare time to care for others and it was taking a toll on Lilah's emotional well-being, leaving her emotionally brittle, volatile and reactive. Lilah came to me after hearing about the shifts a friend had experienced through my work. She was wide eyed and incredibly curious. Helping her to understand her gifts and natural aptitude to love gave Lilah a newfound respect for herself. Knowing she was empathic helped her to see why she was so good at meeting the needs of others and also explained why she preferred to avoid her own feelings. An empath realises early on that they feel better when the people around them feel better. So, naturally, they believe that helping others is the fastest and easiest way to ensure they feel good.

Unfortunately, not everyone wants to feel better and so an empath can feel stranded and powerless if she continues to think she can influence her own emotional state by first bringing love to another.

Empowered empathy is when we become devoted to bringing love, attention and devotion to our own inner emotional world, while also imparting it to others to whom we feel inspired and led. Together we began by turning Lilah's loving heart in on itself. Supporting Lilah to find ways to enjoy her own company, reflect on her own feelings and pay attention to herself brought new confidence, rejuvenation and awareness. Lilah could see how she had actually never ever been truly 'with' herself. She began to take care of herself in the ways she needed to. Getting enough sleep, eating well and regular exercise was a given. Beyond this, recognising what she was feeling, reflecting on what she could sense within and devoting herself to a life that brought her joy and fulfilment created a totally new perspective.

The more Lilah paid attention to her feelings, the calmer and more grounded she became, until she noticed a clear pattern emerging. Any time Lilah was around her friends who had partners, she began to feel jealous. She would cringe at the sight of loving couples, whether she was at a wedding or trying to unwind with a romantic comedy at home. She found herself reacting on an instinctive level and feeling emotionally out of control.

Together we brought loving awareness to her desire for love. An eruption of tears came forward when I suggested that Lilah was reacting because she secretly desired love for herself. It was difficult to acknowledge, but it did help her to understand her recent emotional reactions – all the triggers pointed to the same thing.

Lilah had only ever been in one relationship, many years previously. While she was not ready to date, she was ready to accept the truth of what her heart longed for and begin seeking ways to show up for herself daily in love, so that she felt heard, cared for and listened to.

Lilah didn't feel as though men really cared for her. She saw and believed that other women could attract men so easily. It was time to play some new games, to support Lilah in discovering a whole new experience with men. I invited her to forget about the gender of those in front of her and instead focus on a man's heart; genuinely caring for her companion and intently finding out about his life, dreams and current circumstances. Lilah's loving heart could be generous with friends, family and strangers, but when it came to men she found it hard to be herself. Playing with this new challenge initially created apprehension and fear, as this was a totally new perspective for Lilah. She began to practice this new game with co-workers and quickly experienced something very new; when she showed that she sincerely cared about the lives of the men in front of her, they reciprocated and were truly interested in asking about her life as well. Rich, open, enjoyable conversations with men created a whole new dynamic with the opposite sex for Lilah.

It was time for dating, and with her new skills in hand and an open heart she found a new ease in connecting with the opposite sex. It wasn't long before Lilah had attracted an adoring boyfriend who appreciated her, found her attractive and genuinely cared about her. Lilah was astonished. However, even after dating for a few months she found herself too scared to fully open to her boyfriend's love. Lilah wanted to really give herself permission to be herself and receive his love wholeheartedly.

Together we returned to her first relationship. Lilah had just left home and had found herself naturally drawn to Trevor, who was generous with his compliments and knew how to treat her in a way that demonstrated how much he cared. She loved loving Trevor, and even though she compromised and didn't honour herself, she figured enduring a little discomfort in the name of love was a worthy self-sacrifice. Receiving love from a man for the first time was profound for Lilah, and she quickly gave her power away by finding ways to please and serve her man to ensure his affection didn't wane or dwindle. Reflecting on this past love brought a sweeping recognition that Lilah had been subtly betraying herself in an attempt to keep her old boyfriend's love alive. A cathartic emotional surge erupted within, as Lilah saw the cause behind her pattern.

Being able to recall her willingness to set her own needs aside, dull her soul expression and mute her concerns and needs left the relationship lacklustre. Lilah was now able to see her desire to love without being loved and this epiphany gave her full permission to open her heart and allow herself to be vulnerable enough to receive. To let herself be herself, ask for what she wanted and stand in a willingness to truly receive, for what was actually the first time in her life.

It's fascinating to see what we believe we need to be and do in order to be worthy of love. I love to be a lover, just like all of the women I devote myself to. Being in the giving position is our strength and servicing the emotional needs of others while neglecting our own is a long held tradition among women of all cultures and backgrounds. As we seek to give without receiving, we steal love from ourselves. We incriminate the act of receiving and cut ourselves off from what we think we want to generously supply others with. True love is a balancing act of reciprocating love; sometimes we should be the giver and at other times we need to be the receiver. Some blessed moments are a unique tangle of both sides of the delicious exchange of love. Stepping into the vulnerability of allowing ourselves to receive opens our hearts to the most blessed experience of all; being in love together. We can see the love we have for others truly taken in by them, and still feel it flow and fill us simultaneously.

# Healing Guidance

1. In what relationship have you been trying to give love, while blocking your flow to receive love?

2. Identify one person you trust in your life right now whom you feel ready to courageously receive love from?

3. If you find it challenging to be loving towards men, young children, the elderly, or your in-laws etc., give yourself permission to see them as infinite souls worthy of love. Enquire about their day, find out what brings them joy and discover the lovability of a new sector of humanity.

## Visualisation:

*To bring loving awareness to the heart, allow yourself to see rich emerald green swirling beautifully around your heart area.*

| *Wounded perspective* | *Healed perspective* |
|---|---|
| I don't know love | I love freely |
| Love is weakness | Receiving love supports me |
| There is not enough love | I give generously and receive plenty |

# Healing Affirmations

- I am worthy of the investment of love

- My capacity to love expands as I receive

- True love is a reciprocation of care and devotion

- Every soul is worthy of love

- I extend love and feel loved in return

# Chapter 9 – Fulfil Desire

*Wherever*

*you go,*

*go with*

*all your*

*heart.*

*Confucius*

*The solar plexus is the home of our will, emotions, desires and sense of personal power. Our will and desire to create is held within the same area in which we hold the power to bring intention into form. The solar plexus is the area most connected to our inner world of emotion - can you imagine all of our feelings, desires, intentions and will being located in the one power centre? It helps to clarify why being disconnected from how we feel unknowingly disconnects us from our desires and power to create what we want - Being able to lovingly receive, witness and transmute every emotion that moves through our form is imperative for us to be able to live in our power and create the experiences that we truly yearn for.*

Karen and I had been in contact for a few years and on the day we finally met at one of my live events we both felt an unmistakable connection. Karen knew that I could see within her, and while it felt exposing, it also felt relieving. Having someone who comprehends and understands us can be a liberating step in accepting who we really are and allowing ourselves to acknowledge the truth of what is happening in our own inner world.

Beautiful, well spoken and kind hearted, Karen and I felt drawn to work together. Karen was experiencing a swell of emotional volatility that affected her daily, finding it tiring to try to keep up appearances and fulfil her work responsibilities. Her inner world seemed to be constantly experiencing a storm of unknown origin.

Karen was an interesting and outwardly well-rounded woman - successful in her career, with a love for dogs and having travelled quite extensively in her life. Even so, we were quickly able to reveal the extent and causes of the emotional turmoil, when Karen was given the space to really open up and share; she was able to see how key events from her past were creating an emotional burden that was unbearably heavy to carry every day. Losing her first partner, the passing of loved ones, a feeling of disconnection from her own family and bitterness towards her brother were all creating turbulence that was disrupting her ability to function on a day by day basis.

The intention to heal was a permission slip to begin to look at how the past was a real and formative experience in her life. The level of pain and strain these historic events had created for Karen's emotional world was completely demanding her attention, to a point at which she had to peer within and be willing to face the discomfort; continuing any further in the same way was simply no longer possible. Our connection allowed Karen to begin processing and transmuting the experiences from her past in perfect order, ushering in a profound catharsis that brought continual relief for Karen.

Within her tummy, her solar plexus was a battlefield strewn with fears of failure, the repression of genuine desires, and the heavy grievances of holding herself to blame for not having what she wanted most in life. Moving through the layers of self-resentment gave her passage to the bedrock foundation of pain at the root of it all; not trusting her own power. Karen actually knew that she was incredibly connected, gifted and intuitive, and that scared her more than all of her pain combined.

One by one her soul brought forward experiences of grief that had directed Karen to give away her power. Walking away from her first love meant that she turned off her ability to give and receive love freely from her heart chakra. Feeling betrayed by someone who she had hoped she could rely on had left Karen feeling as though she couldn't really trust even those closest to her – causing root chakra damage. As Karen bravely peered into the darkness and asked in faith for her truth to be restored, she was led to uncover a wealth of revelations. Visions confirmed sacred elements of her truth and light poured in, reminding Karen of who she truly was. A deep connection with spirit in her crown chakra, amazing perception in her third eye, and a willingness to speak truth opened up Karen's world to love once more.

This insight changed the whole way Karen operated. Shifting

into a receptive position of acceptance in which she could gradually come to allow her own power to be was a liberating leap, making a fundamental difference in what she was capable of creating for herself in her own life. After months of feeling run down and uninspired by her work, she knew this revelation confirmed it was time to launch her own business. It had been safe for Karen to invest her skills and expertise in others, rather than utilising it independently to grant herself access to the wealth, freedom and self-reliance she desired.

The truth was that Karen was always aware of what she truly desired - she just never gave herself permission to own that it was possible, because that would mean actually being seen, actually rising in purpose and being willing to take off the shroud of shame that had caused her to dim her own light.

She was able to really observe the shadow teachings from her Mother and see how her Mother had given her own power away, by denying her gifts and sensuality and waiting for others to grant her what she secretly wished for. Never actually receiving what she truly wanted – despite it being unspoken and hidden - gave her Mother permission to stay in the martyr position and spend her life complaining and regretting what could have been, if only someone else would have done x, y or z. Being able to use this shadow example of personal power was the call to purpose that Karen needed to accept the discomfort of doing something completely new.

The first string of clients confirmed Karen's capacity to serve and from then she focussed on growing, refining and choosing the work that lifted her. Calling on her genius, Karen aligned her plan for wealth and really started to see the confirmation that she did have the capacity and opportunity to create what she desired. Karen was facing a choice now - to own her power or to choose to sabotage it. But the truth is that seeing how we truly operate within gives us ample resource to judge and condemn ourselves, or to wash ourselves deeply in compassion and mercy. Karen was able to use the pain of acknowledging her fear of her power to turn to the heavens and to be led and shown a new way.

In one healing session, Karen was able to visualise the generations of powerful, connected and intuitive women in her ancestral line who had been hunted, ridiculed and ostracised because of their power and their gifts. Seeing this vision gave Karen permission to see that in her own life she had the opportunity to honour her ancestors, by choosing to be willing to step into her power and claim her magnificence in a way no other women in her family history had been able to do. Being able to see the chance, the choice and the possibilities to rise up and allow herself to exhibit and utilise her own power was exhilarating; Karen was able to grant herself access to all of the things she truly desired, in a stand for herself and her ancestors that sent tingles cascading over her whole body.

We often fear that looking within will be terrifying and painful, confirming that what is there is beyond our capacity to face. But life rewards the brave, and the more we peer within to truly comprehend how our past pain has cultivated, blessed and refined us gives us access to powerful information that we can use for ascension. It permits us to rise, not because that is what we desire, but because the pain of choosing not to is greater than we can bear.

# Healing Guidance

1. What emotion have you been avoiding feeling most this last month?

2. Allow yourself to know when it's the right time to journal out your sincere feelings. Writing, bringing awareness and creating acknowledgements will lift and clear your solar plexus.

3. Write down the top 10 things that you are truly grateful for in your life right now. Now write down the top 10 things that you desire the most in your life right now.

## Visualisation:

*To bring loving awareness to your solar plexus, allow yourself to see golden sunflower yellow swirling beautifully around your naval area.*

| *Wounded perspective* | *Healed perspective* |
|---|---|
| **I can't create what I want** | **I own my power** |
| **I'm lost** | **I know what I want** |
| **I'm not allowed what I want** | **I desire what's intended for me** |

# Healing Affirmations

- I bring loving awareness to every feeling within

- I honour all feelings and feel them lighten and release

- I have the power to create everything I desire

- I am safe in my power

- I use my power wisely to bless my life and the lives of others

# Chapter 10 -

# Own

# Divinity

*Beyond the waves of your mind shines
the light of your divine presence.*

*Author unknown*

*Grieving the love that we've lost causes a forgetfulness to wash over us. In an attempt to once again seek love, we can be too willing to accept counterfeit love in an attempt to numb our pain. Our sacral chakra is the area of our creativity, sensuality and connection with our procreative energy. When our sacral chakra is damaged, our ability to recall our own divinity and trust our creative and sensual expression can become distorted.*

Josephine is someone who gives deeply and freely. As a teacher for a special needs class, Josephine devotes herself to the precise and rigorous requirements of her classroom bringing compassion, mercy and kindness in lavish quantities. Her success and fulfilment as a teacher comes from her willingness to invest in others what she was not shown personally.

Josephine came to me seeking a way out of her own shadow patterns; a ten month string of one night stands had left her feeling shameful, unwanted and hopeless. In her professional life, she was renowned for being caring and generous but in her personal life she felt deeply unlovable. Josephine was afraid that she would never find love and couldn't seem to stop herself from seeking it in these random sexual rendezvous, even though she knew that they were not serving her.

Together we clarified the purity of her desire to seek love, and also confirmed how her shadow pattern was taking her further and further away from any real, meaningful experience of the love she yearned for.

Josephine's Mother had miscarried a baby only months before conceiving Josephine. The loss and grief of losing one baby had prevented her Mother from truly being able to embrace and receive her living daughter and had initiated her own descent into grief, leaving little to give to the young Josephine. This pattern of with-holding love had, understandably, confused and upset Josephine and left her with deep ongoing concerns about her own lovability.

Josephine's generously loving nature was an aspect that her school peers found strange and undesirable and Josephine was frequently left out, betrayed and abandoned by some of the other children. Interestingly, despite the social rejection Josephine faced, she still chose to embrace and deepen her loving nature all the more, finding others who had also been rejected and choosing to invest her powerful love into them.

All of us are intuitively drawn to those whom we feel an affinity with; we are all attracted intuitively to the people whose wounds reflect our own. We never like to see another suffer in any way similar to how we ourselves have suffered. Josephine was able to reflect on her own early years of being a generous loving friend, she could see how she was so willing to give to others what she had not received, but even that knowledge and realisation did not hit the spot. She still didn't truly feel connected to her peers.

Now, as an adult, Josephine had mastered the art of giving what she hadn't been shown, but knew it was time to discover the power of investing love in herself. Josephine realised that the censured love she had been shown had inadvertently activated her purpose. Being able to see her own wounding clearly gave Josephine a deep respect for herself and a sense of acknowledgment around her own suffering. What we can't see and perceive remains unacknowledged, and while unacknowledged, we continue to descend and fall deeper into darkness.

It only took a single episode of doubt for Josephine to once again seek love through a one night stand. She experienced a turn of events that left her feeling so worthless and disgusted in herself that it felt as though her light had extinguished. The abyss of hopelessness seemed to engulf her, as she admitted to herself that she didn't know how to feel loved. The pain was so intense that it finally caught her attention! Josephine knew she had to change, but she had no idea what to do or how to do it.

All of us are exposed to this grief, a lack of love that wounds us and drives our behaviour as we seek the one thing we all desperately need. Josephine had found her purpose in giving what she didn't receive, but was still blinded by her subconscious drive to experience love through sex. Compulsive one night stands and feeling unloved by her Mother seem unrelated, but it's the heart pain within that confirmed the connection between these two seemingly disparate aspects of Josephine's life. Bringing healing to this area for Josephine involved acknowledging the depth of what she had suffered personally, as we cannot heal what we have not witnessed within. Josephine already held her Mother in deep compassion and while she had forgiven her, Josephine had internalised the perceived rejection and had unknowingly chosen to replicate it in her relationship with herself. It was Josephine's own rejection of herself that was at the core of this wounding; a refusal to hold herself in love and instead seek it outside of herself was at the root of her promiscuity.

Bringing loving awareness to this secret pattern within was the flush of truth that allowed Josephine to begin reclaiming her power. Clearly seeing that one night stands only brought further damage to her sacral chakra created the space for Josephine to uncover her own capacity to invest love within herself. Her generous affirmation, acknowledgement and compassion now had a new recipient and the effect was profound. Slowly and surely, the more Josephine showed up for herself and treated herself with loving kindness, the more light and free she began to feel. Her pattern of one night stands melted away as she acknowledged her desire for a real relationship.

After much trepidation, Josephine started dating. While she was adept at embarking upon sexually intimate relations with a man, she was unsure about how to actually invest herself emotionally in a genuine conversation with a potential partner! However, before long she was dating someone she felt a connection with; they laughed, had fun and enjoyed each others' company. But as soon as the topic of intimacy arose, Josephine quickly shut down the conversation and refused to participate in any dialogue. Mirroring this refusal, the man she was dating backed away and they decided to stop seeing each other. Josephine shared what had happened with me and I encouraged her to actually return to the conversation and ask if they could both speak together honestly, even if they decided not to restart the relationship. He agreed to meet with her and for the first time in her life, Josephine actually confided in another human being. She shared her fears around intimacy because of the experiences she's just moved away from. Seemingly miraculously, her companion reflected her vulnerable heart share and relayed his own beliefs about not feeling loved in the relationship if she didn't want to be intimate with him. It was brutal, pure honesty; true heartfelt expression, a vulnerably daring act from both of them which was pivotal in Josephine's healing. To share her feelings and needs, and have them acknowledged and received, was a turning point for Josephine. The pair decided to continue dating and after they had both braved a series of open, revealing conversations, their love, appreciation and affection for one another grew and before long they were engaged.

Josephine was astonished to see how learning to both give and receive love through honest heartfelt communication was the key to realising that love was available to her. She allowed herself to feel the wash of knowing that being committed to speaking her truth and honouring her sensuality could bring healing. Her bravery gave Josephine access to finally see and embrace the world of love that she had been seeking her whole life.

# Healing Guidance

1. Write down the first three words you think of when you ponder your own sensuality and sexuality.

2. Are there behaviours or people related to your intimate life that it's time to forgive? May I suggest writing a 'Self Audit' Healing Love Letter (from the Appendix) to release the past and free yourself to find peace and comfort in your innate sensuality.

3. What is one simple thing you could do to deepen your relationship and trust with your own sensuality?
*(i.e. Look at your whole naked body with love the next time you take a shower/bath, apply lotion to your whole body lovingly and gently or receive a facial or back massage to honour your beautiful body.)*

### *Visualisation:*

*To bring loving awareness to your sacral chakra allow yourself to see warm deep orange swirling beautifully around your vaginal area.*

| *Wounded perspective* | *Healed perspective* |
| --- | --- |
| I am disgusting | I am divinely sensual |
| It's wrong to be desirable | I embrace my sensuality |
| Sex is dirty and bad | I find bliss in sexual embrace |

# Healing Affirmations

- I see the wonder in my naked beauty

- I am connected to creative energy through intimacy

- My sensuality is a reflection of my divinity

- I enjoy the bliss and surrender of sexual union

- Sexuality allows me to explore my divinity

# Chapter 11 –

# Find

# Home

*Everyone wants to be cradled in care by those surrounding them, and feel safe knowing we belong where we are. When we don't find the deeply accepting, supporting full embrace of love we were hoping for early on, we begin a quest to discover its true origin, source and location. Root chakra wounding involves feeling unsafe and out of place in this world, even within our own body. Until we can feel the security of knowing that we truly belong at home within ourselves, we will continually seek love, affection and acceptance from those outside of us. Opening to the confirmation from above that we truly belong within our own souls brings a calm sense of knowing that all is well and as it should be.*

P iper had a fabulous sense of humour and knew how to laugh off emotional discomfort. A joy to be near, her effervescent personality was able to lift, support and delight you at every turn. Piper had become an expert at emotional manipulation, as she didn't want anyone in her presence feeling left out, ignored or judged in any way. She could sense if you weren't feeling like a part of the group, and would effortlessly use her innate gift for humour to reconnect you, so that you felt like an important part of the team.

Piper's artistry and dedication to inclusion had rich roots, as she had faced years of feeling like a strange misfit that didn't really belong anywhere. She came to me incapable of swimming within the enormity of her own inner emotional world. Proficient at lifting and including others, Piper felt out of control within her own body, indulging in eating frenzies and couch-bound movie marathons; a sense that she was incredibly broken haunted her life.

Single and unhappy, most days felt too big for Piper. Being able to find a love that supported and nourished her felt hopeless, as nothing vaguely approaching this had ever been a part of her life. She desperately feared that the dream of love she yearned for was just a mirage that she needed to relinquish. We came together to help her heal the past, so that she could finally find real love.

Piper's life had taught her not to ask for more and accept what little she'd been given. The eldest in a family of 8, her parents were busy and Piper had to shoulder a level of responsibility few of her age know. Feeling unable to request what she desired, Piper entered adulthood without a sense of security and the knowledge that she was safe and watched over. Her first boyfriend came along and swept her off her feet; they were soon married and suddenly Piper had two step-children and entered Motherhood with swift speed. The love that started her relationship seemed to grow weaker and thinner as each day passed.

Subtle undercurrents of subversion and attack became increasingly visible. Piper's body became as scrutinized as her sexual desirability. Months passed as subtle put-downs increased to outright attacks, and devastated by what was happening, Piper spiralled into a sea of hopelessness and sadness. Inevitably the relationship deteriorated to a point where it was not sustainable. Piper found herself single and deeply confused and hurt by the whole experience. Her greatest fears that she was unlovable seemed validated by her marriage break-up.

Together, we were able to look into Piper's relationship with men prior to meeting her ex-husband and witness a series of concessions that laid the foundation for what she would accept in her future. Not feeling good enough to earn her Father's approval had left a wound that made her future husband's behaviour seem acceptable. Feeling unlovable, as though she somehow did not qualify for her Father's approval, was verified in marriage - this time, by her husband. Torrents of tears flowed as Piper was able to grieve the loss she had never been aware of as a young woman. She had never felt as though she had a Father; in fact, she realised that she had almost become a sort of Father figure to her 7 siblings. Piper could now see that even as a grown woman, she was overwhelmed by trying to make sure her siblings were safe and had what they needed, even though she still didn't feel safe within herself. Piper progressed as she had space to mourn her loss and grieve the descent that she'd known. Acknowledging her empathic gift gave even more understanding to the life experiences she had encountered. Establishing boundaries and supportive self-care practices allowed Piper to find a sense of empowerment and hope.

Piper was brave and willing to face whatever was necessary in order to bring healing. She courageously chose to open a daring conversation with her Dad, seeking to gain a better understanding of their relationship. She relayed how much effort she put in to win her Father's approval, and how she had never felt as though it was enough to make him proud. This vulnerable heart-share was met with complete surprise, as Piper's Father apologised and relayed how unaware he had been that she had ever felt this way. He hugged Piper, held her close and boomed deeply his great appreciation for his beautiful daughter, expressing how incredibly proud he truly was of her for everything she had accomplished.

Piper had received clarity that rocked her world. After being brave enough to request an intimate conversation with her Father and reveal her deep sense of not belonging, she could now heal as she opened to the truth that she was loved; she could sit in the sense of security she needed. Healing confirmation from her Grandfather who had passed away years previously reiterated how incredibly precious, loved and infinitely cared for Piper was.

It was time for love; time to start dating. After decades of feeling as though she wasn't good enough, it was time to embrace herself with deep compassion and complete acceptance. Piper took her whole soul to the dance floor and shook her delectably self accepted body with wild care-free abandon. Her liberated lotus energy provoked a flurry of response from the surrounding single men. They could sense that this woman was reclaiming her power and they were drawn in by the deep allure of what she was accessing. She was able to show herself more clearly and openly than ever before. Sebastian, an incredibly tall, gentle hearted and resolute gentleman, was drawn in by the Aphrodite-like sensual power Piper exuded.

Piper was fully at home in self love and committed to viewing the whole planet as a place of love, which allowed her to see it everywhere she went. Sebastian was different to any man she had previously encountered, with a sensitivity and gentleness that she had not encountered before. So grateful to have Piper in his life, Sebastian would honour her and treat her with the highest respect at every turn. Opening doors, cooking vegan meals and bringing the most comforting accepting space she had even known ushered in a new experience of truly feeling at home.

Piper was able to realise that her wounds had deeply affected her ability to feel safe and protected. The lack and suffering that invariably befalls us all, has a way of affecting how we see life, how we see love and how we see ourselves. The courage to challenge long held assumptions about who she was and what she deserved was paramount for Piper in being able to heal and clear her perception. Finally feeling at home within herself allowed her to behold the wonder and magic of a world filled with hidden love. While tempting to slip into judgements and fear, Piper can now hold herself in compassion as she remembers the truth that love is all there is.

# Healing Guidance

1. How safe do you feel in your life? Rate the level of safety you feel in your life between 1-10, with 10 being completely safe and calm and 0 being no sense of safety at all.

2. Reflect on your relationship with your Mother and Father and identify whether you can feel any unmet needs creating a sense of not being safe within you. Turn to The Parent Audit in the Appendix and trust yourself to create a Healing Love Letter to your Mother or Father, or use The Self Audit Healing Love Letter framework to support you to in healing your root chakra.

3. Say a prayer and ask for confirmation that where you are is exactly where you are meant to be in your life right now. Ask and pray for confirmation that you can turn to the heavens for support, guidance and protection, to help you feel safe and cared for.

**Visualisation:**

*To bring loving awareness to your root chakra, allow yourself to see deep red swirling beautifully around the lowest section of your spine or very bottom of your bottom.*

| *Wounded perspective* | *Healed perspective* |
|---|---|
| I'm not safe | I am safe at home in love |
| I don't belong here | I am at home in my soul |
| I don't fit in | I belong here |

# Healing Affirmations

- I am exactly where I need to be

- I am cocooned in divine love and protection

- Universal care envelops me

- The Divine Father provides for me and protects me

- I allow myself to feel deeply held in loving embrace

# Chapter 12 -

# Heavenly

# Connection

*The more light you allow within you,*
*the brighter the world you live in will be.*

*Shakti Gawain*

*Finding ourselves restored to divine heavenly connection ushers in a wave of healing truth that is vital for our ascension. Our crown chakra is the place where we begin life with full access to the heavens; we know we are bathed in divine light, guidance and love. We will all go through a stage of losing connection with this brilliant source of love and reassurance. In an attempt to replace this sense of love and connection, we search tirelessly for a way to feel held, nurtured and bathed in deep embrace. The crown chakra wound is often forged early in life and leaves us with little recollection of divine love. If one chakra is crucial for our divine purpose, it is definitely our crown chakra – the access point for all truth.*

C amilla could not recall ever having this divine connection. We met through a mutual friend and began working together to support Camilla with her relationship with her 10 year old Daughter. Emotional turmoil showed up easily in the hearts of both Camilla and her Daughter Emily. Both highly sensitive empaths, Emily was being raised by her single mum, Camilla, and both were doing their very best to love, support and care for each other. Emotional wobbles in one heart would ricochet and show consequential ripples in the other.

Camilla only wanted her Daughter to feel safe, supported and emotionally secure within. I reassured Camilla that learning to develop this for herself would automatically ensure that her Daughter felt, received and knew the same as well. So our work began, motivated by a Mother's desire to support her Daughter.

Firstly, to abate the emotional volatility that Camilla had become accustomed to, we brought loving awareness within. Learning how to sense, name and bring loving acceptance to her own inner feelings was a completely new skill set. Camilla was brought up to hide, ignore and fear her own feelings. Her empathic gift was unrecognised. She had decades of experience in making herself "wrong" in order to fit into the family she was born into. Now, decades later, her own sensitivity was being mirrored back to her by her own Daughter and she knew she needed to take action to prevent her Daughter from experiencing anything similar to the pain that Camilla knew.

Journaling was a powerful tool and Camilla quickly found her way to accepting her inner emotional world, with the practice soothing and calming the seas within. The next step was to make herself a bigger priority in her own life. Time away from home with girlfriends had been dismissed as 'unimportant', because staying at home with Emily would always take precedence. Turning the tides to permit herself some adult time with girlfriends brought resistance from her Daughter, as Emily feared she may end up becoming less important on her Mother's list of priorities. Together we supported Camilla with vocabulary to ensure Emily felt safe, important and deeply cared for. A new depth of honesty in their conversations came forward as Camilla learnt to express her own needs with her Daughter. After just one night out visiting girlfriends, Camilla was feeling so much better, having seen how she had gone against the resistance to put herself first. The buzz in her heart confirmed it was a step in the right direction.

Quickly Emily followed suit, taking more care of herself too, by making more of her own meals and complaining less when Mummy wanted to go out. The two were creating an improved relationship where Camilla was modelling the self-love and self-care that she longed to establish and see in her daughter. This became the catalyst for Emily to treat herself with a new level of kindness and consideration to match her mother's new investment in herself. Camilla was entranced by the changes she witnessed in her Daughter and allowed herself to step deeper into the work we were enjoying together.

Camilla had no animosity towards her parents for their lack of understanding for her gifts and innate emotional sensitivity. Caring for her parents was such a huge part of her life; she had already found deep acceptance in knowing they did their very best. Being able to emotionally soothe, comfort and bring harmony to arguments was the super-human gift that Camilla's suffering had forged within her. Being easily triggered by loud voices and disagreements, Camilla's confident negotiating and conflict defusing capacity had ample opportunity in the difficult relationships she bore witness to. And yet, while she could bring more calm, peace and harmony to those around her through loving leadership, Camilla had no idea how to find peace within herself.

One particularly powerful healing session unfolded when Camilla was intuitively guided back to a time when she was quite young and her mother was unwell. Her Mother was laying down with severe cramps. Blood stained sheets had just been removed to be washed by loving neighbours, while her Father was desperately on the phone calling the ambulance. Camilla stood alone before her Mother, witnessing her deep pain, and a sense of powerlessness washed over the young girl. In that moment of commotion and fear Camilla believed that her Mum would not live. When her Mother was whisked away, Camilla fell into the despair and mourning of a Daughter who had just lost her Mother.

Camilla's Mother received the care she needed and made a full recovery. She eventually came home and all was apparently well. Nothing 'bad' had happened and the family was all back together. There was no discussion around what had unfolded or how Camilla had felt about the whole experience. Camilla was able to reflect back to witness the feelings in her internal 'little girl'; she recognised that in the moment her Father was calling the ambulance, she had not only feared losing her Mother, but had felt as though her Mother had actually died, when she was taken away from her in the ambulance. Camilla was able to recall that as a child, once her Mother had returned home and was OK, she had vowed to never let anything happen to her Mother again that would jeopardise her life. While it's impossible to prevent illness, death and accidents, Camilla could now recognise that she had made herself responsible for her Mother's safety and protection – an incredibly heavy burden for a little girl to bear. Now, as an adult, that promise to protect her Mother had engulfed her relationships with everyone in her life. She felt responsible to care and protect for all of them; her Daughter, her co-workers and her friends, let alone her aging parents.

Camilla could finally see that she was losing so much energy and vitality by trying to control something completely beyond her power. In order for Camilla to heal this false perception of what she was responsible for, she needed to connect with those who truly do have power. I said a prayer and asked that Camilla be able to see, perceive and know the loving energies, angels and guides that surround her. Tingles and peace confirmed for Camilla the presence of one particularly caring guide. She couldn't exactly see him or hear him, but the love, warmth and protection he brought was palpable and washed her all over with tingles. Camilla basked in the warm rays of this divine love and felt her whole soul soothed by this potent heavenly love that confirmed she was indeed watched over and protected. This revelation naturally brought a tide of healing shifts.

With my help, Camilla recognised that we are all watched over and guided by heavenly beings whether we know, accept or even want it or not. This experience gave her permission to lean into the care that was available for her and trust that everyone close to her was also being held in divine love too – relieving her of the burden of sole responsibility.

Giving ourselves permission to connect with our own experience of the divine is deeply restorative. As we let in heavenly love, we let in a wave of truth that can heal, restore and nurture us. We have all faced events that have left wounds and which have created unnatural responses that cause us more pain. This pain is an invitation to surrender and turn to the heavens for help, love and guidance to find our truth and embody our divine purpose.

Since accepting a once dormant desire to pursue leadership,

Camilla has felt far more free and and much more energized. She knows that she has the power to create a life that will fulfil her, now that she has clearer boundaries around what she needs to invest herself in and where the parameters of her responsibility finish.

# Healing Guidance

1. How guided and protected do you feel in your life? Rate your level of connection from 1-10, with 10 being the strongest, most continual connection and 0 being no connection at all.

2. Recall 3 moments in your life when you knew you were being guided, protected or blessed by the heavens.

3. Write in your journal, "Divine Guidance" and allow yourself to write down 5 of the most recent little whispers or flashing glaring signs that have come into your life recently. Thank the heavens for being a part of your beautiful life.

## Visualisation:

*To bring loving awareness to your crown chakra, allow yourself to see deep purple swirling beautifully around the top section of the crown of your head.*

| *Wounded perspective* | *Healed perspective* |
|---|---|
| **I'm shut-off and alone** | **I am open to receive** |
| **I'm afraid of myself** | **I am divine** |
| **No one can help me** | **I am guided at every turn** |

# Healing Affirmations

- I am held in divine care

- I am surrounded by beings who care deeply for me

- I allow myself to feel and perceive those near to me

- Continual access to guidance is mine

- I bask in the joy of deep heavenly connection

# Chapter 13 - Goddess Ascension

Love is

all there is

Emily Dickinson

*This is the sacred story of Lysa, the goddess of exuberance. The story of how she fell into grief and unknowingly gave away her power. She allowed herself to lose her light before reclaiming it and ascending from the depths to rise in divine purpose.*

After feeling deeply unloved by her own Mother, the still young Lysa was heartbroken and stricken with grief. Her repeated advances toward men failed and Lysa was left feeling deeply depressed and hopeless. She decided to seek love in the kingdom of the underworld, a place ruled by her Ego and fears.

Lysa began her descent into the kingdom of the underworld seeking the love she yearned for. Within that dark place stood seven walls with seven gates. Lysa cried out "Let me in".

The guardian of the gate, Nadu, peered over at her. "Open this gate, or I will break it down and scream so wildly you'll fear for your own life" Lysa demanded.

Nadu, the guardian of the gate replied "Please don't break down the gate, let me take your request to her Majesty Ego of Lysa, Queen of the Kingdom of No Love. Wait until I return".

When Lysa's ego received word of her sister's request she was enraged. "How dare she come down into my kingdom? I'll teach her a lesson" and Queen Ego decreed that Nadu grant Lysa passage into the underworld.

Nadu returned and unbolted the locks and opened the first gate saying "You may enter the realm of Queen Ego, fine lady. Welcome to the place from which no one returns" and as he spoke he took Lysa's ability to feel guided.

"Why are you telling me I can't trust the signs and signals of heavenly guidance?" Lysa asked.

"Tis the wish of Queen Ego. You may only enter if you submit to her rule" Nadu explained and Lysa bent her head and passed through the first gate. Shortly she came to the second gate and once again Nadu unlocked the bolts and opened the second gate. He removed her ability to speak her truth and Lysa asked "What are you doing telling me that I cannot share the truth of who I really am?" Nadu replied, "Tis the wish of Queen Ego, you may only enter if you submit to her rule."

Once again Nadu unlocked the third gate and removed Lysa's capacity to love deeply declaring "Tis the wish of Queen Ego, you may only enter if you stop being so deeply loving."

At the fourth gate Nadu granted her access only by removing her connection to her inner world of feelings and innate desires; forcing her to surrender any hope that she could ever create a life filled with love. Lysa passed through but once again at the fifth gate, Nadu required Lysa to surrender her divine sensuality - she had to reject her sexuality completely. At the sixth gate, Nadu removed Lysa's ability to feel safe in the world, and at the seventh gate, passage was granted only as Lysa was stripped of all heavenly connection. Lysa had lost all of her truth and now stood exposed, completely naked.

She had entered the realm of Queen Ego and stood bewildered before her sister, Queen of the Kingdom of No Love. Behind Ego's throne emanated lifelessness, there was no light and no hope. The extinguished dreams and abandoned hopes were all dressed in black feathers resembling ominous birds. Lysa became frightened, wishing she had not come to this dark place in search of love. Her quest was hopeless and now she was trapped, desperately she bowed before her Ego pleading for her freedom. Ego replied, "You are in my realm now. No one returns from my Kingdom of No Love. The gates are already bolted behind you!"

Ego sent forth a venomous snake to transform Lysa into a lifeless black bird. With one venomous bite, Lysa became covered in black feathers, obliterating her exuberant expression and tender desires; within moments the light from her eyes extinguished as all of her memories and hope for love disappeared.

Above on the earth, a great change came as Lysa's light was lost in the underworld. Honest expression, the freedom to be exactly who we are and the exuberance to believe everything is possible ceased in woman and animal in the absence of the goddess. Birds ceased to sing, bulls no longer frolicked freely, stallions lost a remembrance of the joy of galloping, and rams cared not for delicious grass. Women ceased to shine in their authentic light.

Shamash, the Sun God, was deeply troubled by what he saw. He knew of the disaster that would ensue if exuberance ceased; it was only a matter of time. While Shamash knew his power could not rival Ego's strength, he turned to Ea, the Great God and shared how earth's creatures were no longer rejoicing. Ea decided to form Udush, a creature devoid of any emotion or fear, to act as a powerful emissary to restore Lysa and return exuberance to earth. Ea sent Udush deep into the underworld where he effortlessly passed through the seven gates much to the surprise of Nadu. He stood in the court of Queen Ego "I am here for Lysa, the Goddess of Exuberance".

Ego stood and screamed, attempting to scare and curse Udush, but her powers were no match for the Great God Ea and Udush withstood the blow unaffected. Ego was bound to submit and she brought forth Lysa covered in black feathers. All watched as Udush administered the waters of life, sprinkling it over the black feathers. They saw her transform back to her natural form.

Lysa was restored; however, she was weaker than a new born babe. She remained faint and pale, bent over, bowing before Ego.

She had life once more. Udush guided her through the darkness as she ascended through each of the seven gates. Nadu saw Lysa feebly drawing near and reminded her that she can call on the heavens at any time and guided her through the seventh gate. At the sixth gate he reminded her that she truly does belong and can feel safe and at home within her own soul. At the fifth gate she remembered that her innate sensuality was a part of her divine identity, as was her ability to know she could create anything she desired. Nadu returned Lysa's permission to love others deeply at the third gate, and her precious ability to speak her truth at the second. Back at the first gate, Lysa bent her head down and Nadu reminded her that she has the capacity to see truth and the all encompassing presence of divine love and she arose returned to her full glory with renewed life and power.

As Lysa came forward from the cave entrance to walk upon the earth the birds broke out in song, the stallion galloped wild and free, the bull frolicked over clover clad fields, and rams went in search of the sweetest grass. Women everywhere arose in wild acclaim remembering the power of simply being who they are; all of creation rejoiced.

# The Ascension of Goddess

## of Goddess

_____

*(insert your name)*

*This is the sacred story of* _____ *(insert your name), the goddess of* _____ *(insert the name of something magical you bring). The story of how she fell into grief and unknowingly gave away her power. She allowed herself to lose her light before reclaiming it and ascending from the depths to rise in divine purpose.*

After_____ *(insert your grief or loss)*, the still young _____ *(insert your name)* was heartbroken and stricken with grief. Her repeated advances toward _____ *(insert how you sought love)* failed and _____ *(insert your name)* was left feeling deeply depressed and hopeless. She decided to seek love in the kingdom of the underworld, a place ruled by her ego and fears.

_____ *(insert your name)* began her descent into the kingdom of the underworld seeking the love she yearned for. Within that dark place stood seven walls with seven gates. _____ *(insert your name)* cried out "Let me in".

The guardian of the gate, Nadu, peered over at her. "Open this gate, or I will break it down and scream so wildly you'll fear for your own life" _____ *(insert your name)* demanded.

Nadu, the guardian of the gate replied "Please don't break down the gate, let me take your request to her majesty Ego of _____ *(insert your name)*, Queen of the Kingdom of No Love. Wait until I return".

When _____'s *(insert your name)* ego received word of her sister's request she was enraged. "How dare she come down into my kingdom? I'll teach her a lesson" and Queen Ego decreed that Nadu grant _____ *(insert your name)* passage into the underworld.

Nadu returned and unbolted the locks and opened the first gate saying "You may enter the realm of Queen Ego, fine lady. Welcome to the place from which no one returns" and as he spoke he took _____ 's *(insert your name)* ability to feel guided.

"Why are you telling me I can't trust the signs and signals of heavenly guidance?" _____ *(insert your name)* asked.

"Tis the wish of Queen Ego. You may only enter if you submit to her rule" Nadu explained and _____ *(insert your name)* bent her head and passed through the first gate. Shortly she came to the second gate and once again Nadu unlocked the bolts and opened the second gate. He removed her ability to speak her truth and _____ *(insert your name)* asked "What are you doing telling me that I cannot share the truth of who I really am?"

Nadu replied, "Tis the wish of Queen Ego, you may only enter if you submit to her rule."

Once again Nadu unlocked the third gate and removed _____ 's *(insert your name)* capacity to love deeply declaring "Tis the wish of Queen Ego, you may only enter if you stop being so deeply loving."

At the fourth gate, Nadu granted her access only by removing her connection to her inner world of feelings and innate desires; forcing her to surrender any hope that she could ever create a life filled with love. _____ *(insert your name)* passed through and once again at the fifth gate, Nadu required _____ *(insert your name)* to surrender her divine sensuality - she had to reject her sexuality completely. At the sixth gate, Nadu removed _____ 's *(insert your name)* ability to feel safe in the world, and at the seventh gate, passage was granted only as _____ *(insert your name)* was stripped of all heavenly connection.

_____ *(insert your name)* had lost all of her truth and now stood exposed, completely naked.

She had entered the realm of Queen Ego and stood bewildered before her sister, Queen of the Kingdom of No Love. Behind Ego's throne emanated lifelessness; there was no light and no hope. The extinguished dreams and abandoned hopes were all dressed in black feathers resembling ominous birds.

_____ *(insert your name)* became frightened, wishing she had not come to this dark place in search of love. Her quest was hopeless and now she was trapped. Desperately she bowed before her Ego pleading for her freedom. Ego replied, "You are in my realm now. No one returns from my kingdom of no love. The gates are already bolted behind you!"

Ego sent forth a venomous snake to transform _____ *(insert your name)* into a lifeless black bird. With one venomous bite, _____ *(insert your name)* became covered in black feathers, just like all of her _____ *(insert the name of something magical you bring)*; within moments the light from her eyes extinguished as all of her memories and hope for love went out.

Above on the earth, a great change came as _____'s *(insert your name)* light was lost in the underworld. _____ *(insert the name of something magical you bring)* ceased in woman and animal in the absence of the goddess. Birds ceased to _____ *(insert your own expression)*, bulls no longer _____ *(insert your own expression)*, stallions lost _____ *(insert your own expression)*, and rams _____ *(insert your own expression)*. Women ceased to _____ *(insert the name of something magical you bring)*.

Shamash, the Sun God, was deeply troubled by what he saw. He knew of the disaster that would ensue if _____ *(insert the name of something magical you bring)* ceased; it was only a matter of time. While Shamash knew his power could not rival Ego's strength, he turned to Ea, the Great God, and shared how earth's creatures were no longer _____ *(insert the expression of something magical you bring)*. Ea decided to form Udush, a creature devoid of any emotion or fear, to act as a powerful emissary to restore _____ *(insert your name)* and return _____ *(insert the name of something magical you bring)* to earth. Ea sent Udush deep into the underworld where he effortlessly passed through the seven gates, much to the surprise of Nadu. He stood in the court of Queen Ego.

"I am here for _____ *(insert your name)*, the Goddess of _____ *(insert the name of something magical you bring)*". Ego stood and screamed, attempting to scare and curse Udush, but her powers were no match for the great God Ea and Udush withstood the blow unaffected. Ego was bound to submit and she brought forth _____ *(insert your name)* covered in black feathers. All watched as Udush administered the waters of life, sprinkling it over the black feathers. They saw her transform back to her natural form.

_____ *(insert your name)* was restored, but was weaker than a new born babe. She remained faint and pale, bent over bowing before Ego. She had life once more. Udush guided her through the darkness as she ascended through each of the seven gates. Nadu saw _____ *(insert your name)* feebly drawing near and reminded her that she can call on the heavens at any time before guiding her through the seventh gate. At the sixth gate, she remembered that she truly does belong and can feel safe at home within her own soul. At the fifth gate she recalled that her innate sensuality was a part of her divine identity, as was her ability to know she could create anything she desired.

Nadu returned _____'s *(insert your name)*

permission to love others deeply at the third gate, and her precious ability to speak and share her truth at the second. Back at the first gate, _____ *(insert your name)* bent her head down and Nadu returned to her the capacity to see truth and the all encompassing presence of divine love and she arose returned to her full glory with renewed life and power.

As _____ *(insert your name)* came forward from the cave entrance to walk upon the earth the birds _____ *(insert your own expression)*, the stallion _____ *(insert your own expression)*, the bull _____ *(insert your own expression)*, and rams _____ *(insert your own expression)*. Women everywhere _____ *(insert your own expression of the magic that you bring)*; all of creation rejoiced.

# Appendix

LYSA BLACK

Your task is not to seek for love, but merely to seek and find all the barriers within yourself that you have built against it.


Rumi

If you are anything like me, you've waited a long time for approval, acceptance, recognition or love from your parents or your lovers... and even if you get a bit, or a lot... it never really hits the spot, right?! Or maybe you've had to earn it... or maybe you've never even had any of it!

The truth is we know their wounds, we know their story... and yet we wish, we wait and we hope that they will give us what we know we need.

The world of emotion is my forte and I have created 3 simple yet deeply powerful 6 question Healing Love Letters: **'The Parent Audit'**, **'The Ex Audit'** and **'The Self Audit'** to support you through a process in which you can release, acknowledge and forgive the people required to reclaim your power.

These are letters you will never send and need never be seen or witnessed by anyone else but you.

I promise you that in giving yourself the space, the permission and the freedom to express yourself honestly here, you will unlock a reservoir of wisdom, power and truth that you need to step into all that you are.

It was my own debilitating self-doubt, fear and self-criticism that called me to pay attention to my relationship with both of my parents, my past boyfriends and myself.

I am here to honour you for being brave and willing to step

into the discomfort - and maybe, for the first time, be present to acknowledging how you feel about your relationships with these key people in your life.

I want you to know that I trust you to find the courage and kindness within yourself to show up and be with the answers that flow through your pen. You can allow your heart to release what it has feared to express for so long.

This is not so much about them, but about you... and I am here to invite you to establish a new relationship with yourself. One which starts with a promise to now show up and offer yourself what these people didn't, couldn't or wouldn't.

I assure you that giving yourself what you never got will be the healing balm that will support you to step more fully into your power, purpose and peace.

I honour your experience and hold deep trust that something magical, beautiful and magnificent can birth from what you have experienced.

It is time to Ascend.

# The Parent Audit

Name of your Parent *(Mother, Father or Primary Caregiver)*:

_____

What can you honour and appreciate this parent for - no matter how small/ grand or seemingly insignificant?

1.

2.

3.

What can you see about this parent now that was invisible to you 10 years ago?

1.

2.

3.

What are the three major ways that your parent most hurt you or let you down?

1.

2.

3.

What three things did you not receive from this parent that you know it's time to start giving to yourself?

1.

2.

3.

Who have you become because of this parent's example?

1.

2.

3.

What are three things you can genuinely thank your parent for now?

1.

2.

3.

# The Ex Audit

Name of your Ex:

_____

What do you wish you could have said to your Ex when you broke up?

1.

2.

3.

How did your Ex hurt you?

1.

2.

3.

How did your Ex help you?

1.

2.

3.

What blessings came from your time with your Ex?

1.

2.

3.

What can you forgive yourself for from your time with your Ex?

1.

2.

3.

What have you changed since your time with your Ex?

1.

2.

3.

## The Self Audit

Your full name:

_____

What 3 things do you honestly need to admit to yourself right now?

1.

2.

3.

What do you know you need to let go of in your life right now?

1.

2.

3.

What three mistakes do you know you need to now forgive yourself for?

1.

2.

3.

What three things is it time to dedicate and commit yourself to? *(i.e. self-care, journaling, saving money, speaking the truth etc.)*

1.

2.

3.

What three desires can you feel calling to you from your heart?

1.

2.

3.

What are three judgements against yourself that are you ready to release? *(i.e. "I'm stupid", "I'm unworthy", "I'm not worth loving" etc.)*

1.

2.

3.

One of the oldest and most generous tricks that the universe plays on human beings is to bury strange jewels within us all, and then stand back to see if we can ever find them.

Elizabeth Gilbert

# About The Author

*Lysa Black* is a Heart Healer. Dedicating 10 years to healing her own heart opened Lysa to her natural gift of healing presence. Being intuitively guided to heal her own anxiety, binge eating and pattern of break-ups led Lysa to her soul purpose. She is a highly sensitive empath who has the superpower of 'reading' hearts; Lysa can relay information about your current and past emotional experiences, life theme's and patterns as well as spiritual gifts and soul purpose. Author of *Heart Healing* and *Divine Purpose,* Lysa's open heart, self-acceptance and compassionate presence creates an atmosphere where others can access their own inner healer. She has professionally stood besides thousands of clients over a span of 8 years; she is an internationally sought after guide and mentor for those seeking to authentically align in purpose as Healers and Leaders. Lysa lives with her husband and two young children in Northland, New Zealand.

**See Lysa:**

Facebook: https://www.facebook.com/EmpressLysaBlack/

Instagram: https://www.instagram.com/empresslysablack/

YouTube: https://www.youtube.com/c/LysaBlack

Website: http://www.lysablack.com/

www.ingramcontent.com/pod-product-compliance
Lightning Source LLC
Chambersburg PA
CBHW071430090426
42737CB00011B/1621